Breaking New Ground for SLIFE

Breaking New Ground for SLIFE

The Mutually Adaptive Learning Paradigm

Second Edition

Andrea DeCapua & Helaine W. Marshall

University of Michigan Press
Ann Arbor

Published in the United States of America by the
University of Michigan Press
Manufactured in the United States of America
Printed on acid-free paper

ISBN 978-0-472-03933-3 (print)
ISBN 978-0-472-22120-2 (e-book)

First published May 2023

Contents

Acknowledgements

We wish to thank the following colleagues, students, friends, and family members who have been instrumental in helping us with this second edition of *Breaking New Ground*. First, we thank the classroom teachers who graciously shared their MALP projects with us: Yasmeen Coaxum, Beth Evans, Renee Finneran, Lesly Garcia, Danielle Golub, Kathryn Mercury, and Judith Zivan. We are indebted to both Dr. Anita Bright and Dr. Jill Watson, who contributed their innovative materials and activities for further exploration for our chapter on adolescent learners. In addition, we thank the teachers who provided access to their classrooms and whose lessons and activities are described in our book: Carol Antolini, Elizabeth Cicero, Ann Hoskins, Ann Marie Keinz, Martha McGloin, Erika Perez, Madeleine Reyes, and Gloria Rodriguez. Nicole Nguyen and Son Ngoc Pham are two of the many students who willingly shared their work with us. We also thank the anonymous reviewers who enriched our work with their valuable insights and perspectives.

Finally, we especially appreciate the contribution of Hugh Marshall, who read the entire manuscript for clarity and consistency.

List of Figures

Introduction

A Culturally Responsive and Sustaining Instructional Approach—The Mutually Adaptive Learning Paradigm

In this second edition of *Breaking New Ground,* we have incorporated many new features that reflect both our current thinking based on recent research, and continual work with classroom teachers of students with limited or interrupted formal education (SLIFE), a subpopulation of English learners (ELs). This book, like the first edition, introduces a pedagogical approach designed especially for SLIFE, who share certain characteristics that set them apart from other ELs, regardless of their level of English proficiency. We call this approach the Mutually Adaptive Learning Paradigm, or MALP, because it incorporates students' home languages and cultures, embracing their backgrounds as a foundation for instruction, rather than as an enhancement or addition.

New in this second edition is the division into two parts. Part One focuses on (1) describing SLIFE as learners who generally come from primarily oral backgrounds, hold collectivistic orientations, and have primarily experienced learning outside of formal education; and (2) introducing MALP and providing sample lessons analyzed using the MALP Teacher Planning Checklist, which has been revised for this edition. Part Two, with almost completely new and reworked material, focuses on MALP projects created and implemented by real teachers in their classrooms.

Organization of This Book

In Part One of this book, we introduce the culturally responsive and sustaining instructional approach, the Mutually Adaptive Learning Paradigm® (MALP®). This approach provides teachers with a framework for understanding what will work and why (DeCapua & Marshall, 2011; Marshall & DeCapua, 2013; Marshall, DeCapua & Antolini, 2010).

We begin in Chapter 1 by exploring assumptions about teaching and learning and how these are shaped by culture and literacy practices. Readers are encouraged to engage in the various Discovery Activities, designed to help them better understand their own cultural lenses, as well as those of SLIFE.

Chapter 2 builds on Chapter 1 by investigating the two different learning paradigms, that of SLIFE and that of formal education. Here we consider how prior learning experiences within various sociocultural contexts influence how people understand, interpret, and interact in the world around them, including in school.

With Chapters 1 and 2 providing the foundation, in Chapter 3 we present the Mutually Adaptive Learning Paradigm (MALP). We will have seen that SLIFE and educators in Western-style formal education systems hold, for the most part, very different assumptions about teaching and learning. MALP makes these different assumptions explicit. Because MALP is mutually adaptive, the instructional approach requires both parties, SLIFE and educators, to recognize each other's critical priorities so that SLIFE can transition to the practices and expectations of formal education.

The last chapter in Part One, Chapter 4, details how two teachers implement MALP by intentionally and consistently infusing it into their instruction—Christina in her social studies class, and Rick in his math class. This chapter also introduces the MALP Teacher Planning Checklist (introduced in the first edition, but since revised), and shows step by step how Christina and Rick used it in planning and reflecting on their projects and lessons.

In Part Two, we move into actual SLIFE classrooms and look at how to implement MALP by presenting projects from MALP-trained teachers. Along with the detailed steps of these projects, we also provide samples of completed MALP Teacher Planning Checklists to illustrate how a particular project aligns with the elements of the MALP approach.

First, in Chapter 5, we discuss projects in general, and then consider what specifically makes a project a MALP project. We conclude the chapter by describing in detail one MALP project, called The Mystery Bag, an example of the Class Collections type of project. In The Mystery Bag project, we see how SLIFE practice three academic ways of thinking—categorization, compare and contrast, and defining.

Next, in Chapter 6, we present another type of MALP Project, Class Surveys, where students learn about data collection, analysis, and reporting skills. This project can be adapted to different student groups depending on the topics and questions selected for the survey. These two project types, Class Collections (using The Mystery Bag example) and Class Surveys, demonstrate how MALP can prepare SLIFE for academic work in formal education.

Then, in Chapters 7 and 8, we introduce six projects designed and delivered by current MALP-trained instructors in the field. The projects in Chapter 7 are designed for young learners, and those in Chapter 8 for adolescent learners. While the projects as outlined here are tailored to specific age groups, each one can be adapted by altering the language and content to make them appropriate for various ages.

The final chapter, Chapter 9, concludes this second edition by reflecting on the journey made by one teacher. We include sample lessons from this teacher both before and after she received training in MALP. In this chapter, we also reexamine the cultural assumptions underlying teaching and learning. Finally, readers will find observations from a former SLIFE who was successful in making the transition to formal education.

Terminology

SLIFE

Educators and researchers have not formed a consensus around a single term for this subpopulation of ELs. In both editions of this book, we have adopted the acronym SLIFE—Students with Limited or Interrupted Formal Education, first used by DeCapua, Smathers & Tang (2009). Although the appropriateness of this acronym has been questioned (see e.g., Browder, Pentón Herrera & Franco, 2022), we believe that it draws attention to the factors that distinguish these learners from other ELs. We also believe that it is important not to subsume SLIFE within the other ELs, because the former face additional challenges in formal educational settings that the latter do not.

As reflected in the term SLIFE, regardless of ethnicity, country of origin, or native language, all of these students enter the school system with little or no exposure to formal education, which may or may not have been interrupted, hence the inclusion of the descriptor "limited" along with "interrupted." The lack of prior exposure has unfortunately led to SLIFE at the secondary level being among those students at the highest risk of dropping out (Davila, 2012; Lukes, 2021; Montero, Newmaster & Ledger, 2014).

Regarding the use of the term SLIFE in this book, given that the "S" in SLIFE stands for students, we do not refer to SLIFE as either "*SLIFE students" or "*SLIFE learners," but rather simply as SLIFE or the SLIFE subpopulation.

Literacy

As regards the term "literacy," we recognize that there have been developments in the field of education and the meaning of literacy that have expanded this term to include not only print or text-based literacy, but also the many other types of literacies used to communicate through oral, visual, and other modes of expression. UNESCO, for example, states:

> [b]eyond its conventional concept as a set of reading, writing and counting skills, literacy is now understood as a means of identification, understanding, interpretation, creation, and communication in an increasingly digital, text-mediated, information-rich and fast-changing world. (https://en.unesco.org/themes/literacy)

In addition, UNESCO acknowledges the concept of multiple literacies:

> the assumption that individuals 'read' the world and make sense of information by means other than traditional reading and writing. These multiliteracies include linguistic, visual, audio, spatial, and gestural ways of meaning-making. Central to the concept of multiple literacies is the belief that individuals in a modern society need to learn how to construct knowledge from multiple sources and modes of representation. (http://www.ibe.unesco.org/en/glossary-curriculum-terminology/m/multiple-literacies)

While acknowledging this broader understanding of literacy, in this book we adopt the term literacy in its narrower meaning of reading and writing print materials, whether hard copy or digital. Print literacy is required for academic achievement as dictated by mandated curriculum, instruction, and assessment. As such, reading and writing skills must receive dedicated attention if SLIFE are to succeed in the current educational system.

We further recognize the existence of significant structural barriers and systemic inequalities in education—including those around the understanding of literacy itself—as means of exerting power and maintaining societal hierarchies (see e.g., Gandara, 2020; Gonzales & Shields, 2015; Harklau, 2016; Linville & Pentón Herrera, 2022; Tourse, Hamilton-Mason & Wewiorski, 2018; Zhao, 2016). We affirm that these sociopolitical issues must be addressed in the long term as part of comprehensive educational reform. For the purposes of this book, however, we take a more immediate and pressing view: Students currently in school need to complete their education under the existing system, which demands that SLIFE master the requisite reading and writing skills in a relatively short time span.

What we do address in our work is the need for a culturally responsive and sustaining approach to education for SLIFE, one that meets students in the middle rather than demanding that they conform in all respects to a new and unfamiliar formal classroom setting. To accomplish this, we ask teachers to make a paradigm shift in the direction of their students to make learning more accessible. The details of this mutual adaptation, The Mutually Adaptive Learning Paradigm (MALP) are presented in this book. We believe that this shift will be an important first step in moving away from a *deficit* view of SLIFE to one of *difference*.

In sum, *Breaking New Ground, 2nd edition,* guides readers to a deeper understanding of the SLIFE subpopulation. In so doing, it introduces readers to an innovative instructional approach, fosters their knowledge of the academic needs of their students, and provides them with a pathway to addressing those needs using MALP-infused instruction.

Part One

1. Culture, Literacy, and Learning

Educators all have views on what constitutes a strong student, with certain qualities that at first glance seem to imply that they are likely to do well in school. We are going to examine some of those views in this chapter. Before going any further, complete the following activity.

Discovery Activity: What is a Good Student?

Take a few moments to think about your views on this issue.
1. Write two to three sentences briefly describing what you believe makes a good student and how you think students learn best.
2. Put your statements aside where you can easily access them later.

SLIFE are commonly viewed as language learners who have had very little to no exposure to reading and writing in any language, and who have been unable to participate in age-appropriate formal education. However, many other English learners (ELs) can also be understood as SLIFE—that is, struggling language learners of diverse backgrounds who also share the lack of opportunity to engage in age-appropriate formal education. What differentiates the SLIFE subpopulation of language learners from other ELs is their need to build print literacy skills, acquire foundational content knowledge, and develop academic ways of thinking and learning, in addition to developing English language proficiency.

Therefore, it is useful to think of SLIFE as ELs whose experiences range on a continuum—from those who have never attended school, and have never developed reading and writing skills in any language, to those who have been in school, but for one reason or another, their learning environments did not foster the development of age-appropriate reading and writing skills, content knowledge, or an understanding of how to "do" school. Between these two types, we identify other SLIFE, depending on their prior learning experiences and a host of other factors, such as interruptions because of war, civil conflict, natural disasters, or migration. Still others may have attended school until it became necessary for them to leave to take care of family members, or to work to help support their families (DeCapua, Marshall & Tang, 2020).

A lack of basic school resources, with a concomitant emphasis on rote learning, insufficient teacher preparation, and inconsistent attendance contribute to students receiving limited or no age-appropriate formal education, prior to entering our classrooms (Flaitz, 2018). Generally speaking, in such contexts, teachers write information on a chalkboard that students then copy into their notebooks or onto slates or whiteboards (DeCapua, Marshall & Tang, 2020; DeCapua, Smathers & Tang, 2009). Education that focused on rote learning and memorization most likely will not have prepared students for the academic ways of thinking—including, importantly, academic-style critical thinking—that form the basis of the activities conducted in formal educational settings in the so-called "Western style" of instruction. While in their own cultural contexts, these students may have flourished, they find it difficult to function well in this new learning environment. In this book, therefore, the term *formal education* will be understood to refer to this Western style, which is prevalent worldwide in the places where we find SLIFE (Anderson-Levitt, 2003).

Once we understand that SLIFE range along a continuum of prior learning experiences, we realize how difficult it can be at times to determine whether an EL is a SLIFE. When language learners have had no schooling and have no text-based literacy skills, it is clear that they are SLIFE, but for those ELs who have had some schooling and have already developed basic reading and writing skills, it can be a complex process to identify whether they are indeed SLIFE. There may be learning disabilities, trauma, or other factors involved, as discussed extensively in DeCapua, Marshall & Tang, 2020. Nevertheless, it is important to identify SLIFE because this subpopulation of language learners has a cultural orientation to learning significantly different than that of other ELs, given their prior learning experiences outside of formal education. When we recognize that SLIFE, regardless of their prior learning experiences, confront additional challenges beyond those of other ELs, we are more likely to become culturally responsive and culturally sustaining educators as proposed in this book.

This first chapter explores the implications for educating SLIFE in K–12 formal educational settings as found in North America, Europe, Australia, and many other parts of the globe. The perspective taken here is a cultural one. We firmly believe that the cultural dimension has all too often been either neglected, or acknowledged only at a superficial level, in addressing educational issues.

Yet, we find understanding the cultural dimension to be key in promoting the academic success of SLIFE in formal education. We begin by examining what culture is and considering how culture influences learning. Next, we examine the role of print-based literacy as part of the transition process to formal education, and what this form of literacy means for students who bring an oral orientation to communication and learning. Finally, we look at underlying cultural factors common to these students that impact their ability to benefit from formal education and literacy instruction.

What Is Culture?

Successful teachers understand the interplay of language and culture and how culture influences learning and teaching (Chavajay & Rogoff, 2002; Mejía-Arauz et al., 2018). Participation in one's culture influences patterns of human development. How and what we learn, and what we do with that knowledge, are the result of one's community, cultural practices, and traditions (Legare & Harris, 2016; Nasir et al., 2020).

People generally have a sense of what culture is; yet they often have difficulty defining it, precisely because a large part of what comprises culture is below the level of conscious awareness. Culture is frequently perceived as referring to modes of dress, types of food, ways of greeting, and so on. These features are, however, only the readily visible ones. Culture also encompasses subconscious constructs, such as values, beliefs, norms, and ways of both understanding and interpreting the world around us (DeCapua & Wintergerst, 2016; Triandis 1995; Samovar et al., 2014).

Culture is not something innate, but rather something that is molded through collective and individual experiences (Triandis, 2000). DeCapua & Wintergerst (2016) define culture as "the set of fundamental ideas, practices, and experiences shared by a group of people. Culture can also refer to a set of shared beliefs, norms, and attitudes that are used to guide the behaviors of a group of people, [and] to explain the world around them, and to solve their problem. (p. 14)." These less immediately evident cultural elements can be termed *invisible culture* or *hidden culture*. Taken together, these two parts of culture—visible culture and invisible culture—are often referred to as the *iceberg model of culture* (see Figure 1.1).

Those aspects of culture that are readily apparent and obvious—such as cuisine, architecture, music, clothing, and artifacts—form the part of the iceberg that is visible above water. Those aspects that are below the level of conscious awareness—such as beliefs, values, norms, and assumptions—are the

Culture Model: Tip of the Iceberg

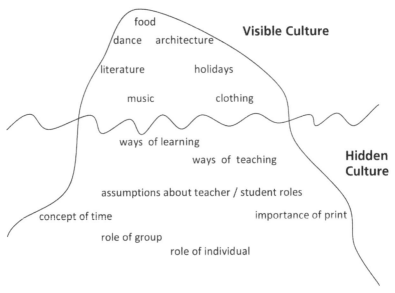

Figure 1.1. The Iceberg Model of Culture

underwater part of the iceberg, and thus are less easily seen. And yet, it is these hidden aspects that affect how members of a culture interpret the world and the behaviors of others around them. They also influence priorities, the nature of relationships, social interactions, and pedagogical practices, both with respect to teaching and to learning (DeCapua & McDonell, 2008). Values, norms, and beliefs lead members of a given cultural group to have worldviews and behaviors that distinguish them from other groups. People generally consider themselves to be members of a group that can be referred to as their primary culture. At the same time, people are also members of myriad subcultures, defined according to any variety of factors, such as ethnicity, region, communities of practices, or social roles. This *intersectionality* exists because we all belong to many cultural communities and are not defined by only one (Lee, Meltzoff & Kuhl, 2022). Despite these subcultural, and certainly individual differences, there are salient cultural features that can and have been identified for specific cultures. Thus, there are fewer within-cultural differences and variations than there are cross-cultural ones (Oyserman, 2017).

In this chapter, we delve into invisible culture to explore three underlying cultural factors we have found that impact how people understand teaching and learning—and that differ significantly for SLIFE as compared with non-SLIFE ELs.

Individualism and Collectivism

We begin this section of Chapter 1 with the following vignette, *The Chopsticks*. Notice here how the father teaches his children about a significant value in their culture:

Discovery Activity: The Chopsticks

1. Read this story and then reflect on it from a cultural perspective.
2. Write your thoughts in a few sentences.

My brother and I were arguing over a trivial issue. We both stormed off, convinced we would never get along, never be friends; we wished the other was never born, or, better yet, adopted, for we wanted no relation to the other. My father, angry, dragged us down to the kitchen table and placed two chopsticks in front of us. He asked us each to choose one and see if we could break it, to which we complied. It was an easy task, breaking a simple stick of wood. Then, though, he bound together four chopsticks with a rubber band, each chopstick representing a member of our immediate family. He handed the chopstick bundle to my brother and dared him to break it. Angered and hot-headed, my brother grabbed the chopsticks and, in a fury, pushed and pulled and wiggled and smashed those chopsticks, but to no avail. One chopstick, my father explained, is very weak, but together, as a family, we could withstand everything. My brother and I nodded in agreement as our anger, for the most part, had passed. At that moment, I believed my father was simply teaching me that I needed to try harder to get along with my brother. Years later, though, this memory has endured, and I realize that this was not simply a lesson for the moment, but a larger cultural value my father was trying to instill in his children. The family unit is more important than our individual selves; it is only through the strength of family that we can achieve and persevere.

—Nicole

Two major cultural constructs relevant to our examination of SLIFE are collectivism and individualism. Cultures can be classified as primarily closer to one or the other category, along a continuum based on the role and priorities of the individual. In collectivistic cultures, people view themselves as integral parts of networks or extended groups. These groups are usually based on kinship but may also be based on clan, religious, or other ties viewed as essential to identifying who belongs to a particular group (Hofstede, 2001). In contrast, people in individualistic cultures view themselves as independent actors focused on their identities as separate individuals (Li, 2012; Triandis, 1994; 1995).

Collectivistic Cultures

In collectivistic cultures, one's membership in a group, the sense of "we together," as illustrated in *The Chopstick*s, is primary. People's sense of who they are, their obligations and responsibilities, the demands placed on them, and their sense of well-being, are strongly influenced by their place and role within their network. Who one is as an individual is not as important as who one is in relationship to everyone else, and commitments to one's network take precedence over individual needs and desires. Since the focus is on the group rather than on the individual, self-actualization, personal attributes, and the accomplishments of an individual for his or her own sake are not central to one's behaviors or identity (Li, 2012). Instead, the actions of an individual are viewed in terms of how they reflect, benefit, or contribute to one's group (Vincent, 2017; Triandis, 2000). Asian and Latin American immigrant adolescents, for instance, are more concerned with their obligations to their families than are mainstream adolescents of European backgrounds (Greenfield & Quiroz, 2013; Trumbull et al., 2020). Mexican parents in the U.S. are often shocked by strict school attendance policies, believing that extended visits to the family's home country during the school year are both justified and necessary for events such as death, illness, celebrating holidays, or other family matters they believe should take precedence over school attendance (Olmedo, 2003).

This alternative viewpoint extends to other areas of formal education. You may have noticed behaviors that are evidence of a collectivistic worldview. Reflect on your experience below.

Discovery Activity: How Collectivism is Manifested in School

1. Describe a situation where a student or students exhibited behaviors that, looking back, might have been closely tied to their sense of collectivism.
2. Discuss this situation with a fellow educator. You might want to start with the following questions:
   - Did the situation surprise you and/or other students? In what way?
   - Did the situation conflict with traditional classroom or school expectations? If yes, how so?

Individualistic Cultures

Members of individualistic cultures give priority to personal goals, efforts, achievements, and independence. A person's identity depends primarily on individual attributes, traits, and accomplishments, and one's sense of well-being centers on self-actualization and one's own performance. Personal judgments and decisions rather than group decisions are the norm. Children, for example, are encouraged to pursue personal interests. Personal responsibility and accountability are paramount, and less emphasis is placed on one's identity as part of a network with mutually reciprocal obligations and responsibilities (Hofstede, 2001).

The following Discovery Activity, *Public Praise*, illustrates a difference in perspective on appropriate teacher behavior between collectivistic and individualistic cultures:

Discovery Activity: Public Praise

The teacher, seeing how much progress Lea has made on her autobiography project, points it out to the other students in the class and tells them that this is really good work, indicating specific content as she praises Lea's efforts. She then suggests that if they have any concerns about doing theirs, they should ask Lea for help. Meanwhile, Lea, embarrassed, keeps her eyes down and, as soon as the bell rings, hurriedly leaves the classroom. The other students leave more slowly, chatting, and laughing with each other.

1. Explain why the teacher's actions appear to be appropriate from her point of view.
2. Explain why they may not have been appropriate from Lea's point of view. Share your comments.

A Continuum—Not a Dichotomy

When discussing individualism and collectivism, we want to keep in mind that these two complex constructs are not mutually exclusive and do not represent a strict dichotomy of cultural differences. Rather, individualism and collectivism should be regarded as a continuum of cultural differences with subcultural differences and variations (Takyi-Amoako & Assié-Lumumba, 2018).

Within any given culture, we can observe elements of both collectivism and individualism (Tyler et al., 2008). No culture is completely homogeneous. Some members of an individualistic culture will more strongly embrace

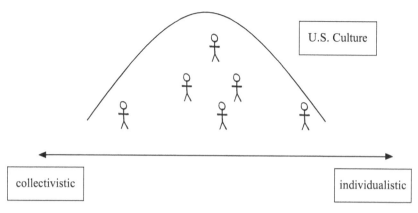

Figure 1.2. A Bell Curve of Culture

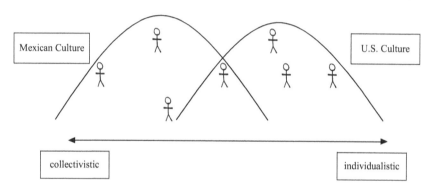

Figure 1.3. The Intersection of Collectivistic and Individualistic Attributes

characteristics of individualism than will others. Nevertheless, as Figure 1.2 demonstrates, in an individualistic culture, the majority of people will have individualistic attributes and in a collectivistic culture, the majority will have collectivistic attributes.

The two overlapping bell-type curves in Figure 1.3 (on page 16) illustrate the nature of this continuum using the examples of the collectivistic culture of Mexico and the individualistic culture of the U.S. The peaks of the two curves represent the largest concentration of individuals in each of the two intersecting cultural categories. For example, members of Mexican or Syrian cultures may typically fall toward the collectivistic end of the continuum, but some may also fall so far toward the individualistic end that they overlap with members of individualistic cultures. The reverse is true for members of Canadian, U.K., or U.S. cultures, who may be at either end of the individualistic range on the continuum.

Care must be taken when applying labels to humans and cultures to avoid overgeneralizing, stereotyping, or essentializing. By this we mean the attribution of specific characteristics to all individuals subsumed within a particular group, race, culture, and/or ethnicity. Despite general salient constructs for the larger notion of culture, it is very important that teachers of SLIFE not lose sight of the fact that their students are individuals as well as members of specific communities and subcultures. Nevertheless, we cannot discount the importance of understanding the cultural divide between individualism and collectivism, and the attendant cultural values influencing the attitudes and assumptions as manifested in accepted classroom practices (Trumbull et al., 2020).

The majority of cultures worldwide range toward the collectivistic end of the continuum (Arevalo, So & McNaughton-Cassill, 2016; Hofstede, 2001). Given that most immigrants and refugees come from collectivistic cultures in Africa, Asia, Latin America, and the Middle East, it is likely that most SLIFE whom teachers will encounter are from collectivistic cultures. Because there are salient cultural values that distinguish collectivistic and individualistic cultures, teachers in countries such as the U.S., Canada, or other Anglo-European countries, may find SLIFE engaging in unexpected behaviors. Consider, by way of example, the concept of cooperative learning. In contemporary pedagogy, cooperative learning is hailed as an effective "best practice" in promoting student engagement and learning for all populations (see, e.g., Ferguson-Patrick, 2020; Gillies, 2016).

Cooperative learning is grounded in basic tenets teachers follow to ensure that group work is carefully structured. As DeCapua & Marshall (2011) point out, this could be considered a collectivistic practice. However, perceptions and understanding of how students are to perform in group settings by teachers in the U.S., reflect the individualism of formal education in individualistic cultures. In such classrooms, although learning that is conducted cooperatively is viewed as a team effort, each person is assigned a specific role or task that, when fulfilled by all the members of the group, completes the group assignment. Each member acts as an individual member of the team and is individually accountable for his or her own learning (Jacobs & Renandya, 2019). In contrast, from a collectivistic viewpoint, when a group functions cooperatively, members reach consensus and share both responsibility and accountability for the group's tasks, without needing to specify individual contributions (Ibarra, 2001).

Mexican culture is far more collectivistic than that of the U.S. or Canada, and has a strong emphasis on the extended familial network so that reciprocal obligations and support and the needs of the family are prioritized when making individual decisions (Martinez, 2016). The term *familismo* is often used to refer to how strongly the family is revered in Mexican culture (Durand, 2011). Other examples of the importance of the family and extended familial network in collectivistic cultures, and the impact these have on students' individual educational goals and choices are the discussions by Farid & McMahan (2004) and Luster et al., (2009) on Sudanese cultures; and Tonui & Mitschke (2020) on the Karen people of Burma (Myanmar).

In families with limited economic resources, children dropping out of school to help the family, whether by working and providing additional income or by caring for younger family members, is not uncommon, reflecting the priority of one's group needs over individual needs or desires.

Discovery Activity: The Chopsticks, Part 2

1. Review the notes you made on *The Chopsticks* (page 13).
2. Share your thoughts.
3. After having read more of this chapter and after your discussion, how have your thoughts changed?
4. How might you use *The Chopsticks* and what have you learned in this section to explain examples of collectivistic behavior to other teachers, administrators, and/or support personnel?

In sum, many of the SLIFE you will have in your classrooms come from collectivistic cultures with very different beliefs, assumptions, and expectations from those in more individualistic cultures. At this juncture, we will now explore SLIFE and print literacy, the most obvious, and arguably, the most visible of factors discussed in this chapter that significantly impact SLIFE as they navigate formal education.

Literacy

You may not have thought of literacy skills as part of culture, except perhaps in terms of the literature of a given culture and/or language. Here we explore literacy as central to the culture of formal education. To begin this inquiry, we ask that you try this activity.

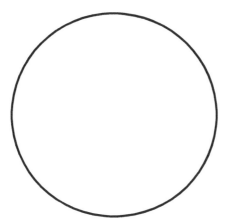

Figure 1.4. Figure of a Circle

Discovery Activity: Two Dimensions or Three?

1. What do you see? Give the first answer that occurs to you.
   - If you said "A circle," you are responding intuitively to this figure as a two-dimensional one.
2. Now move into a three-dimensional space and suggest what you might answer in that context. If you said "The sun," "A ball," or "An orange," you moved quite easily into three dimensions.
3. How do you think SLIFE might respond to this figure? Explain why.

In completing this activity, you were likely able to shift your perspective between the two-dimensional and the three-dimensional interpretations of the figure. For question 3, however, consider whether or not SLIFE would have this same response. In fact, SLIFE exist primarily in the three-dimensional space of the real world. Now think of yourself as a student who lives in this three-dimensional world, and enters our formal education system with its culture of print literacy based on the two-dimensional world of images and print. Rather than concrete, real-world objects, you would be surrounded by images of objects, conversation symbolized by talk bubbles, and written text, rather than oral discourse.

We have started with a distinction between the three-dimensional space of objects and interactions in the real world, and the two-dimensional space of print and images, because the entry into a two-dimensional world is a first step on the road to print literacy. With print literacy comes the ability to understand representational texts, or visual images such as drawings, graphs, clip art, and symbols (Altherr Flores, 2017; DeCapua, 2018; Marshall & DeCapua, 2013).

Teachers regard visual images as standard supports to help learners process information, but understanding images, no matter how realistic they are, is difficult for SLIFE. Images are not real but rather abstract representations of objects, ideas, or signals, or a "code" which SLIFE must learn to interpret. Take, for example, maps. Using a map to find one's way demands making the connection between a two-dimensional interface and a three-dimensional one. For SLIFE, this can be totally new. For someone who has no concept of what a map is, looking at a map of the world is meaningless and appears to be just a random collection of shapes and colors (DeCapua, 2019; DeCapua, Marshall & Tang, 2020).

Even when SLIFE have foundational reading and writing skills, what cartoon images and diagrams are intended to convey may not be obvious to them because they are not the "real" thing. Even for those SLIFE with some schooling in their home countries, their experiences may not have included the types of graphics common in formal education in, for instance, the U.S. or Canada.

Along with their orientation to a three-dimensional world, SLIFE commonly bring with them an oral culture that is rooted in the oral transmission of knowledge. The basics of literacy—letters, sounds, syllables, words, phrases, and sentences—even more than schematic visual representations, can be extremely confusing. Because of their oral backgrounds, they regard language as a continuous flow of sound rather than segments that can be dissected into discrete units.

Even those SLIFE with some reading and writing skills are likely to find using the written word as a means of information exchange or knowledge-building to be demanding, because in formal education the written word is used as a process to learn, as well as a skill in and of itself (DeCapua, 2019). If given a choice, SLIFE will choose oral transmission over the written word to access new ideas or information.

Print literacy is essential and expected, not only in formal education but also in contemporary life in countries in which the written word is evident everywhere. Children, even at very young ages, are frequently exposed to some form of print. Most SLIFE are likely to have come from environments in which reading and writing were not a major priority. SLIFE consider interactions with other people directly through oral transmission their primary resource for knowledge, rather than reading or writing of documents. In their world, there are few or no traditional print materials such as magazines, newspapers, books, flyers, or newsletters; there are rarely computers (Nag et al., 2019), and little to no environmental print such as signs or billboards.

Print literacy skills have embedded themselves so deeply in our formal educational system that it is difficult to conceive of a successful school experience devoid of these skills. SLIFE have learned a great deal in their lives with minimal or no print literacy and have succeeded in becoming learned and competent in many areas. Such knowledge, known as "funds of knowledge," (Moll & Greenberg, 1990) exists in their memories and in those of others they rely on for their expertise. Once in our schools, however, SLIFE must newly master a tool that most of their classmates have been raised to consider essential to formal education: the written word. Learning without this tool— print literacy—is not a viable option. In order to understand this challenge and to appreciate how people view learning through the lens of literacy, we examine the notion of print-based literacy more closely.

Discovery Activity *No Pencils, No Books* shows how reading and writing are more than skills; they are integral parts of our culture, and embracing them is part of the acculturation process of SLIFE to formal education.

Discovery Activity: No Pencils, No Books

Imagine yourself at a professional development event with your colleagues. The speaker has just announced that there will be no printed words either on slides or handouts. Moreover, there will be no note taking. In fact, you have been instructed to put down all writing implements for the duration of the presentation. Finally, no recordings or photos of any kind are permitted during this presentation.
1. How would you feel?
2. Take a moment to write some words to describe your imagined emotional reaction to such a situation.
3. How do you think SLIFE might feel in a similar situation and why?

As teachers, print literacy is deeply embedded in our processes for interacting with information; therefore, in doing *No Pencils, No Books*, you very likely had negative feelings in response to the situation. Even teachers who rely heavily on oral communication still expect visual cues, specifically text or images, as a support. But for SLIFE, oral transmission is the norm. They are not accustomed to turning to print materials as resources. A student once commented to one of us that before coming to the United States, there had never been any need for him to read:

> I live village, nothing for read, no sign, no book. I go school, we read what teacher write but I ask why learn read if no something to read. Here I walk street, everywhere read. Before I no need reading but here everything is read.
> —Sergio, El Salvador

Sergio's experience is a common reaction SLIFE have when coming to a country such as the U.S. or Canada. While the written word may previously have played little or no role in their lives, SLIFE now must not only read, but read to extract meaning. SLIFE need help transitioning from a world based on oral transmission to one based on print.

Although this next student writes about the U.S., the same would be true in other countries. Notice that he doesn't just talk about doing well in school but in doing well in life in general.

> The most importants I have learned about the United States that is a book, newspapers, or notebook and pens. These things are always let me know how to live here. I always remember the books are the most important things for me to learn when I live in the United States.
>
> —Vuong, Vietnam

Discovery Activity: Pause and Reflect

1. Have any of your students expressed similar thoughts to those of Sergio or Vuong?
2. What was your initial reaction? Since reading this chapter, how have your views changed?
3. In light of the discussion of print literacy as presented in the Introduction, how might you address the centrality of the written word in formal educational settings with students such as Sergio and Vuong?
4. Share with your colleagues.

All SLIFE, even those with many years of exposure to some print, arrive in formal classrooms thinking of printed material as distant from their own immediate concerns, and not as a tool for learning or expressing one's thoughts. For many of them, learning to use print-based materials can be frustrating:

> I lived in a small village and didn't attend school. When I arrived at this high school in America I began attending school for the first time in my life. I feel very frustrated. I don't understand any of my teachers, I don't know how to read or write, I don't know the alphabet.
>
> —Yei (Minnesota Department of Children, Families & Learning)

Discovery Activity Review: No Pencils, No Books

1. Compare these quotes from SLIFE to your response to the Discovery Activity *No Pencils, No Books* on page 21.
2. What reactions did you have to the students' quotes?
3. Discuss how your perspective of print literacy and the written word as essential resources contrasts with these students' perspectives.

As we see from the quotes and in reviewing your responses to *No Pencils, No Books*, a major shift is required for SLIFE to think of the written word as a resource and reading and writing as essential skills—a requisite to success for them in their new formal educational setting.

We now turn to an examination of another equally important underlying cultural factor affecting how teaching and learning are viewed, namely, participation in two different modes of learning—informal ways of learning and formal education.

Culture and Learning

> Education and educational systems are about as laden with emotion and as characteristic of a given culture as its language … it seems inconceivable to the average person brought up in one culture that something as basic as [education] could be done any differently from the way they themselves were taught … This is because, in the process of learning they have acquired a long set of tacit conditions and assumptions in which learning is embedded (Hall, 1976, p. 47).

This quote, although several decades old, still resonates today. Culture strongly influences how people learn and what they value as part of learning. A fundamental distinction is the one between informal ways of learning and formal education.

Informal Ways of Learning

For SLIFE, the majority, if not all, of their prior learning experiences have taken place as part of the sociocultural context of daily life within their communities, homes, and work environments. In such settings, learning is concrete and focused on the here and now, and print literacy is not an essential nor necessary part of the learning process. Knowledge is shared orally

(Ong, 1982), and learning follows the apprenticeship or mentor model, whereby observation, imitation, feedback (primarily via demonstration), followed by more observation and imitation, dominate (Mejía-Arauz, Roberts & Rogoff, 2012). The ways of learning in which SLIFE have engaged have led to the development of a learning paradigm dominated by immediate relevance to daily life, relationships among people, orality, and pragmatic tasks with direct, tangible products centered around solving the needs of and developing skills and tasks necessary for daily life. This is what we refer to as *informal ways of learning*.

As mentioned earlier, some SLIFE have participated in formal education for some period of their lives. However, for how long and what that schooling was like will differ significantly from that which we regard as age-appropriate formal education.

Formal Education

In considering the challenge that SLIFE face when encountering formal education, often for the first time, we need to define what is understood by the term *formal education*, often referred to as "Western-style formal education." This type of education occurs within a specific structure—that is, a regulated and standardized school system. It is systematic and highly organized, taking place in a structured setting.

Informal ways of learning, in contrast, take place in response to needs as they come up. Although SLIFE come to our formal educational systems with rich prior learning experiences, they are generally unprepared for the needs and expectations of formal education. For educators to promote the transition of SLIFE to this new way of learning, the first step is to understand the model of formal education in the schools where SLIFE will now find themselves. Formal education rests on certain principles that drive instruction and that influence educators, sometimes without their explicitly realizing that they are so influenced. These principles derive from ways of thinking that, in turn, result in specific cultural perspectives on learning (Rotberg, 2004).

Formal education is centered around print-based literacy, a standardized canon of knowledge, and delivered by highly trained educators in designated settings with attendant conventions and practices. It is built on scientific conventions; communicates knowledge as distinct subject areas, with material broken down into units presented in definite sequences; and uses literacy-based, decontextualized tasks for building and demonstrating mastery. The underpinnings of formal education include observation, reasoning, and analysis (Popkewitz, 2013).

Pragmatic and Academic Ways of Thinking

Notably, formal education is characterized by problem solving on a heuristic level and by abstract reasoning separated from concrete world and real-life experiences (Flynn, 2007). We refer to these types of reasoning as *academic ways of thinking*, demonstrated in the following activity.

Discovery Activity: Finding Similarities

Answer these questions.
1. What do dogs and rabbits have in common?
2. What is a tree?
3. True or False?
   a. Washington, DC is the capital of the U.S.   True   False
   b. Istanbul is the capital of Turkey.   True   False

If your answer to Question 1 was "Mammals," "Fur," "Ears," "Paws," "They're animals," or anything similar, you used abstract, scientific categories of classification. For Question 2, if you answered "Something with a trunk and limbs," or "Something that has branches and leaves," or anything along these lines, you were again defining based on abstract scientific ways of looking at the world. Teachers across disciplines and in all grade levels spend a great deal of time asking students for formal definitions in different variations of "What is X" (Marinellie, 2010; Schleppegrell, 2004), as in Questions 1 and 2. This is a teaching technique common in formal classrooms but unfamiliar to SLIFE. For Question 3, you most likely had no difficulty recognizing how to answer a true/false question, even if you were not necessarily certain of the answer to Question 3b (which is false; it's Ankara).

What the responses to the questions in this activity demonstrate is a familiarity with heuristic thinking, that is, abstract, scientific, or academic reasoning, derived from the fact that readers of this text have spent many years participating successfully in formal education. SLIFE, in contrast, have different ways of looking at and understanding the world. For Question 1, for instance, they may likely respond with something like, "You use a dog to hunt a rabbit," or "People eat dogs and rabbits," or even "They don't have anything in common," because they are focused on the concrete and on functional relationships (Flynn, 2007).

With respect to Question 2, SLIFE often wonder why they are being asked to define something that is obvious. From their pragmatic perspective, trees are everywhere, so what is the point of asking what a tree is. Readers may be familiar with the term "display questions" for this type of elicitation.

Finally, for Question 3, the entire notion of true/false is perplexing. If something is false, why mention it? A false statement is pointless (Lujan, 2008). In addition, since SLIFE are new to the print-based literacy practices of formal education, they expect what they read to be "true" or "correct," otherwise, why should they read it? As products of sixteen-plus years of an educational model that poses such questions routinely, teachers are rarely aware of the cultural assumptions underlying them. From the perspective of formal education, there is an academic way of interpreting the world, which is assumed to be the "right way." Yet, this type of thinking is very different from the pragmatic way of those who have not engaged in such formal learning. As Flynn (2007) observes, at a concrete level, knowing that all toadstools are poisonous, a person finding a toadstool will associate poison with toadstools and therefore avoid them. In addition to being concrete, pragmatic knowledge, this knowledge has immediate and immutable practical real-world relevance: Eat the wrong type of mushroom and it will kill you. Knowing how to classify dogs and rabbits together, on the other hand, is based on an abstract level of thinking derived from scientific classification, i.e., having learned that the class mammal is one characterized by live births, milk-producing mammary glands in females for nourishing the young, and hair. There is no immediate relevance for this knowledge in the K-12 classroom, but part of the formal education process is learning abstraction, logic, and the hypothetical, all of which are detached from real-world applications.

Starting in the earliest grades of elementary school, instruction in formal education revolves around developing specific cognitive processes, i.e., academic ways of thinking, such as categorization, classification, and other abstract thinking, far removed from concrete and pragmatic referents. At even earlier ages, parents often give children sorting toys that begin priming them to focus on specific salient characteristics, such as shape sorters where they must distinguish between different shapes of the same color. Children are already learning that knowledge is not merely experiential but is derived from thinking about the world in certain ways. In a formal educational setting, this type of knowledge and the articulation of it become ends in themselves, something that SLIFE find difficult both to accept and to master.

For SLIFE, coming from informal ways of learning and accustomed to pragmatic ways of thinking, the notion of "knowledge for knowledge's sake" is considered peculiar because for them, learning has immediate, practical, concrete relevance (DeCapua & Marshall, 2010). Children learn by observation and participating in ongoing tasks, thus providing immediate relevance to their learning. They attend to and practice tasks of direct relevance and receive immediate feedback, whether explicit or implicit, from adults or more adept older children (Rogoff, 2014). These tasks include childcare, agricultural

Table 1.1 Pragmatic Knowledge versus Academic Knowledge

Pragmatic Knowledge	Academic Knowledge
Based on experience, often accumulated over generations and passed down orally	Based on logic and the hypothetical
Focused on the concrete, functional	Focused on abstractions—e.g., taxonomies, compare and contrast
Concerned with immediate relevance, benefit to daily life	Future oriented, decontextualized—immediate relevance and benefit not necessarily important
Frequently culture/environment specific, e.g., agricultural or animal husbandry practices within given context; familial and community cooking practices based on availability, as well as traditions	Not tied to specific culture or environment, e g., algebraic equations, definition of a mammal
Changeable in response to immediate needs, environment	Relatively static, based on globally recognized core canon of knowledge

practices, animal husbandry, peddling wares, masonry, artisanal crafts such as weaving, or other tasks important to the family and/or community. Pragmatic ways of thinking and learning contrast with much of formal education where an assumed goal of K–12 instruction is to prepare students for successful future participation in the adult world of work and life (Salden & Hertlein, 2020). Learning is separated from life and delegated to a specific institution, the school. For SLIFE, on the other hand, learning comes through participation in the daily activities of life, and from an early age they observe and join in family and community labors and endeavors. Moreover, learning is not necessarily age-dependent, as is found in formal education, in which learning is divided into age cohorts and corresponding grade levels. Instead, each member of the community begins learning a given task when judged ready by the adults in that community.

Thus, while SLIFE may have much real-world knowledge based on their life experiences and are well able to interpret and organize new knowledge from a pragmatic perspective, unfamiliarity with academic ways of learning and understanding the world disadvantages them in formal classrooms.

Table 1.1 illustrates some of the principal differences between pragmatic knowledge and academic knowledge.

Assumptions Underlying Teaching and Learning

Teachers in Australia, Canada, the U.S., and other countries with Western-style formal educational systems, have developed specific subconscious assumptions about pedagogy, learning, and student and teacher roles, a result of their professional training and their own schooling experiences (Packer & Cole, 2022). Mainstream students, especially by the time they are in secondary school, share similar assumptions.

The following activity provides an opportunity to explore two common assumptions underlying formal education: individualism and academic ways of thinking.

Discovery Activity: Agree or Disagree

Consider these statements and decide whether or not you agree with them. Circle A if you agree. Circle D if you disagree.

1. Students are ready to participate and demonstrate mastery on an individual basis.	A	D
2. The school experience should prepare students for their future.	A	D
3. Students are ready to become independent learners.	A	D
4. Students expect to perform learning tasks for the teacher to evaluate.	A	D
5. Students expect to be individually accountable for their work.	A	D
6. Students are ready to engage in literacy-based, classroom tasks.	A	D
7. Students should be identified individually as performing well and praised for good work.	A	D

Readers who agreed with some or all of these statements are reflecting the cultural assumptions underlying formal education, of which they most likely are a product and in which they are, or will be, participating as an educator. Even in cultures that are more collectivistic, the educational system, particularly in post-colonial countries, often reflects similar expectations and assumptions about teaching and learning (Roofe & Bezzina, 2018; Takyi-Amoako & Assié-Lumumba, 2018). In other words, even for students and educators in collectivist cultures, school often requires more individualistic behaviors. Nevertheless, the assumptions in this Discovery Activity are not universally held and are not the same assumptions that most SLIFE bring to formal classrooms.

Pedagogical theories and practices are rooted in cultural beliefs, norms, values, and assumptions. The teacher as an authority figure and arbiter of knowledge is more common in a culture in which hierarchical roles and respect for authority dominate (Gu, 2010; Triandis, 1995). Returning to the iceberg model of culture, we can see that most of the beliefs, norms, values, and assumptions underlying culture are below the level of conscious awareness. Educators are frequently unaware of how much pedagogical theories and practices are based on fundamental beliefs, and to what extent these pervade education (Kumaravadivelu, 2011; Loughran, 2017). Indeed, the most difficult cultural assumptions and beliefs to examine are those central to one's own culture. In formal education, for example, a popular pedagogical belief is that students should be active participants in their learning. To this point, the technique of having students raise their hands, followed by the teacher calling on them to speak, is perhaps one of the most ubiquitous measures of participation in formal education (Sahlström, 2002; Waring, 2013; 2016). Even when most students do not regularly raise their hands, they are aware that this behavior is praiseworthy. This belief in students as active learners differs from the predominant pedagogical beliefs usually found in traditional collectivistic and hierarchical cultures, such as Cambodian or Chinese culture (Loy & Ye, 2017). In such cultures, pedagogical practices emphasize respect for the authority and wisdom of the teacher. Teachers are seen as repositories of knowledge, and it is their duty to impart this knowledge to their students, whose duty, in turn, is to receive and absorb this knowledge (DeCapua & Wintergerst, 2016). Being a good listener and note-taker is more valued than being a hand-raiser who seeks to take the floor and speak up.

Let's take another example, independent work. For SLIFE, it is often more important to work together to help others accomplish classroom tasks first, before turning their attention to their own tasks. Such behavior often conflicts with the focus on individual accountability and achievement found in formal education (de Souza, 2013). As we saw earlier in our discussion of cooperative learning, teachers expect individual contributions, even in group work where collaboration is fostered. A central assumption of teachers in formal education is that K–12 instruction should produce independent learners—that is, students who know how to learn or gain information on their own, use what they have learned, and be able to apply their knowledge and skills to new learning situations (Krahenbuhl, 2016; Scarino, 2019). Scaffolding, for example, is considered an essential component of effective instruction for all learners. This is the notion that teachers promote learning by providing students with needed support for learning as they engage in school-based tasks and associated academic ways of thinking. As students become more knowledgeable and comfortable with such tasks, and able to engage in academic ways of thinking, the teacher removes this support little by little so that they become independent learners (Walqui, 2006). The concept of the independent learner is closely tied to an individualistic society with an educational system that values learning on one's own.

Table 1.2 Core Values and Practices

Core Value	Representative Pedagogical Practices
K–12 instruction should produce independent learners.	• Scaffolding: provide support for learning as needed, gradually removing the support as students learn to depend on themselves • Asking for assistance or giving assistance only when necessary
Students are individually responsible and accountable for their learning.	• Cooperative work means working together but with each person individually accountable for a specific task, role, and/or product • Individual assessment of material learned, often through standardized tests
School prepares learners for life after school.	• Designing curriculum without intentionally including immediate, real-world relevance

Table 1.2 highlights some of the core values of mainstream education and representative pedagogical practices as found in formal education in countries such as in Canada, the U.K., and the U.S.

As we have seen in this chapter, there are three important underlying cultural differences affecting teaching and learning: (1) the roles of literacy versus oral transmission (orality); (2) collectivism versus individualism; and (3) informal ways of learning versus formal education. The fact that most SLIFE are members of collectivistic cultures and that they have primarily been exposed to informal ways of learning has led to their developing ways of interpreting and relating pragmatically and orally with the world in the here and now. This differs from ways of learning in formal education that focus on literacy, individual accountability, and the development of academic ways of thinking and interacting.

Discovery Activity: What Makes a Good Student, Part 2

At the beginning of this chapter, you wrote two to three sentences about what you think makes a good student.

Go back now to those sentences and, with colleagues, complete the following tasks. Discuss the similarities and differences in your statements.
1. Evaluate to which extent your statements reflect the learning paradigm of formal education.
2. Identify which statements about being a good student might not apply to SLIFE based on what you have read here. Explain why.

Cultural Dissonance

Considering the intersection of the cultural orientations of SLIFE with the expectations and assumptions of formal education, we can predict that

- our schools will be difficult for them.
- engaging in reading and writing will be challenging for SLIFE as these are new processes for them.
- SLIFE will find the individualistic orientation and academic ways of thinking of the formal classroom setting to be disorienting and to create a profound cultural clash.

We use the term *cultural dissonance* to describe the mismatch between home and school when SLIFE, who come from different cultural values and different learning paradigms, encounter the mainstream cultural values and learning paradigm of formal education. This mismatch frequently causes feelings of isolation, confusion, disengagement, and inadequacy (Brewer & McCabe, 2014). The experience of cultural dissonance can have a substantial negative effect on student performance, leading to poor academic achievement and high dropout rates.

To illustrate the extent of this cultural dissonance, let's look at a summary of the major assumptions of teachers and students in formal education. Throughout this book, we explore how, from the perspective of SLIFE, these assumptions about teaching and learning are, for the most part, not valid.

This summary will be familiar to you from Discovery Activity *Agree or Disagree.*

Assumptions of Teachers and Learners

1. The goals of K–12 instruction are to
   a. produce an independent learner; and
   b. prepare the learner for life after schooling.
2. The learner is prepared to
   a. participate and demonstrate mastery on an individual basis; and
   b. engage in print literacy-based, classroom tasks.

SLIFE face cultural dissonance in the classroom, the hallways, the school grounds, and in all aspects of their school experience. Teachers and administrators may be unaware of the complex assumptions that constitute the learning paradigm of formal education. We suggest that this hidden agenda of assumptions about learning, together with more readily visible issues apparent in tasks such as creating and keeping a notebook, is responsible for contributing to the feeling of alienation that SLIFE face daily.

We believe that before any program for SLIFE can be completely successful, it needs to address both the visible and the hidden, underlying issues. This is illustrated in the comments from Janice who details her early experiences with this population in her high school:

> If you take this paper, even with the holes on the left side and the lines, they don't know what's the front, what's the back. They don't even know where to put their name and where to put the date. Sometimes they write their name right next to the date and maybe another time somewhere else. And their name could be anywhere. All their papers are all over. Even when I give them a binder and the tabs and dividers and sit down with them, it takes a long time and some of them don't get it for the longest time. They don't know what to do with the paper, even when I stay after school and help them organize.
>
> —Janice, high school teacher of SLIFE

Janice's comments highlight how unfamiliar even the basics of school are for SLIFE. While it is tempting to focus solely on such immediate and obvious needs of SLIFE, we must keep in mind that these represent the most readily apparent issues and lie on the surface of what constitutes a much deeper problem. Because SLIFE come from a very different learning paradigm, it is incumbent upon us to shift from a *deficit* view of them to a *difference* view; that is, these are students whose learning paradigm is not the same as that of formal education. The goal of this book is to present our culturally responsive and sustaining instructional approach for such students, one that teachers can use to build bridges between pragmatic ways of thinking and academic ways of thinking, to respond to the cultural gap, and, ultimately, to decrease cultural dissonance.

For Further Exploration

1. Go back to the Discovery Activity *Finding Similarities* on page 25. Try to ask at least five different people two of these questions: "What do dogs and rabbits have in common?" and "What is a tree?" How do your results compare to the discussion after this Discovery Activity?
2. If you are a practicing teacher, think about your students. How would you place them along the collectivistic/individualistic continuum based on the examples and information provided throughout the chapter? Compare the results. What trends do you see?
3. Observe a classroom with SLIFE and take notes on the behaviors and interactions of these students. In particular, look for those that illustrate the points made in this chapter about literacy, culture, and formal education. Share your impressions with a partner or in small groups.

2. Two Different Learning Paradigms

Asking someone how they learn is like asking a fish what it knows about water. With the exception of professionals who analyze and research the way students learn, most people cannot characterize their learning or articulate it, especially not as a paradigm. A learning paradigm is a cluster of (primarily unconscious) principles used to organize and understand learning in a given setting. These principles, in turn, are based on a set of what is known as *schemata* that are familiar and comfortable for the learner. We use this notion of a paradigm to further explore how learning is different for SLIFE than for those with a formal education. We have considered the cultural differences from Chapter 1 and configured them as elements of learning that we can place on two contrasting learning paradigms. This paradigm representation clarifies how SLIFE expectations clash with what they find in the classroom when they move into learning environments predicated on formal education.

We begin this chapter by examining a theory that serves as the core of our work: schema theory. Let us show you how a familiar schema and an unfamiliar schema contrast.

Discovery Activity A: Familiar Ways of Thinking

Recite the months of the year to yourself.

Discovery Activity B: Unfamiliar Ways of Thinking

Now recite the months of the year to yourself in alphabetical order.

For Activity A, you probably rattled off *January, February, March, April,* and so on until you reached *December.* For Activity B, you probably were able to recite at least the first few months in alphabetical order, but not without thinking about it for a while or even resorting to writing down the months and then sorting them into alphabetical order. This is an illustration of a *formal schema.*

We have learned to store the months of the year in our brains in chronological order, beginning with the first month of the calendar year and ending with the last one. When we are asked to retrieve them alphabetically, it is difficult to do so, because the request does not match our formal schema (James, 1987).

Formal schemata are ways our brains store information by organizing concepts and knowledge in categories that are shaped by our experiences in the world in which we live and interact (Alderson, 2000; Anderson, 1999). Learning is one such experience and, as such, consists of formal schemata. By extension, then, we see learning as it is exemplified in formal education as based on a set of concepts that can be described as a cluster of *formal schemata*. If one is unfamiliar with these schemata, one may not be able to access or take advantage of the educational opportunities provided. This is similar to what SLIFE face when entering our classrooms. They are entering school systems with very different schemata and do not organize and process information the same way students with age-appropriate formal education have learned to do.

As you will remember, in Chapter 1 we discussed the iceberg metaphor and described how learning includes cultural aspects that lie beneath the surface, that is, that are generally hidden to us. Teaching is an act of cultural transmission (Legare & Harris, 2016). Both SLIFE and teachers have expectations about learning in a classroom setting, expectations which are assumed and not articulated. In this chapter, we look at these expectations from a contrastive perspective, which allows us to observe how cultural dissonance occurs when SLIFE enter our schools and attempt to learn there.

Conceptualizing a Learning Paradigm

Based on our discussion of the SLIFE population and our examination of the close relationship between culture and learning, we can clearly see how a framework for approaching learning would assist us in adequately serving the needs of this at-risk group of students. The conceptualization of learning used in this book comprises three components, each of which contributes to an overall learning paradigm. These three components are: *conditions for learning, processes for learning,* and *activities for learning.* Taken together, the three components can describe the learning experience of SLIFE or those of formal education.

Components of a Learning Paradigm
A. Conditions for learning
B. Processes for learning
C. Activities for learning

Component A, Conditions for Learning, refers to differing underlying expectations about learning and teaching held by both students and their teachers in any given culture or subculture. **Component B**, Processes for Learning, refers to how students gather and retain new information, and how they display their learning. As we will explore in this chapter, these processes differ greatly for SLIFE and for those with formal educations. **Component C,** Activities for Learning, refers to what students do to develop and demonstrate mastery, and reflects how different cultures and subcultures conceive of and interpret the world. Chapter 1 examined how ways of thinking differ depending on whether people have a pragmatic worldview or an academic worldview, the latter a result of participation in formal education.

In this chapter, we investigate the conditions, processes, and activities most closely associated with SLIFE and then compare and contrast these with those commonly present in formal education today. In so doing, we will explore the mismatch between what most SLIFE need and expect in a learning setting, and the reality in terms of what they find in the majority of formal classrooms.

Component A: Conditions for Learning in Two Settings

In discussing cultural differences in Chapter 1, we examined collectivistic cultures from which the majority of SLIFE come. In such cultures, given the primacy of group relationships, and mutual reciprocity and responsibilities, a sense of interconnectedness is primary. This interconnectedness refers to people knowing the members of their group and feeling linked to them on a personal level. In addition, as students coming from pragmatic worlds where learning is concrete and tied to their everyday lives, SLIFE are accustomed to learning that is immediately relevant to the real world. These two conditions—interconnectedness and immediate relevance—form component A. Table 2.1 illustrates the conditions for learning for each of the two learning paradigms.

In sum, what SLIFE find when they enter a formal educational setting is not what they expect, and what they do expect to find is not present in their new setting (Li & Grineva, 2017).

Table 2.1 Component A: Conditions for Learning

SLIFE	Formal Education
Immediate relevance	Future relevance
Interconnectedness	Independence

Discovery Activity: What is Relevance?

1. Take a moment and jot down what "relevance" means to you when thinking about your teaching.
2. Does your thinking change if we add the word "immediate," as in "immediate relevance"? How?

Immediate Relevance versus Future Relevance

This first condition contrasts how the learning paradigms of SLIFE and formal education view the relevance of what is being learned, namely *immediate relevance* versus *future relevance*. The underlying cultural condition is whether one's thinking is grounded in the present or is oriented toward the future. For SLIFE, the first condition they seek is immediate relevance, so that what they learn will be applicable to their lives in the short term. They are used to learning what they need to know when they need to know it, unlike other students with age-appropriate formal education who have been taught for years that school comes first so that when they grow up they will be educated for the world of work. When teachers select material and justify the importance of the curriculum, they unintentionally create cultural dissonance for SLIFE by not taking into account their need to see the immediate relevance of this material and the curriculum to their lives. While many teachers strive to make learning relevant to their students, there is an underlying assumption that doing so is a matter of added interest and motivation. Students understand that ultimately it is not the current relevance that is the priority, but the curriculum itself, which the teacher will build on in their assignments and schoolwork.

The extensive and ongoing goal setting and planning of formal education highlights this future orientation to learning. Much, if not most, of the content that students actually learn is not retained in later years but serves to develop their intellectual tools and broaden their minds. When teachers explain to students that they will need to know something, it is often accompanied by reference to some other future event, such as, "this will help you on the test," or "you need to know this because you'll be learning about [some related topic] later." Course sequences are another example. Like links in a chain, one course prepares students for the next; they will need what they learn today for another class they will take later. Learning is seen as a foundation for future experience, preceding "real" life, rather than paralleling it (Baker & LeTendre, 2005). The "real life" for which students are being prepared may come long after the learning takes place.

For SLIFE, their prior learning experiences took place in contexts where they used what they were learning in the real world to become competent in or to master the skills needed for specific purposes in their environment (Jiménez-Balam, Alcalá & Salgado, 2019). SLIFE are accustomed to learning as they incorporate it into their daily life. For example, care of farm animals, planting of crops, or traditional handicrafts are learned by example and by doing. When a person learns cooking, agriculture, or carpentry skills, the new knowledge is applied at the time of learning. The learner observes, practices, and gets immediate feedback; learning is pragmatic and parallels life (Rogoff, 2014).

Optimal learning situations demand that students be able to see similarities between prior learning and the current situation, as well as being able to use their prior knowledge in new situations (Sousa, 2016). When material is relevant to learners it is more likely that they will be receptive to it and motivated to engage in this transfer. When SLIFE enter formal classrooms, their prior knowledge in many cases does not allow for this transfer, which contributes to their sense of cultural dissonance. Their funds of knowledge are generally not those valued by formal education. The majority, if not all, school curricula is academic in nature, not relevant or related to the pragmatic worldviews of SLIFE, and has no context relative to their lives. This cultural dissonance makes them vulnerable to "educational disadvantage" with consequent negative effects on academic achievement (Patterson, Hale & Stessman, 2007/2008). It also leads to a deficit view of SLIFE by others who see that they are struggling to fully engage with and subsequently master the curriculum. Instead, to address this dissonance and build confidence, teachers must consciously strive to incorporate the pragmatic knowledge of their students and their students' communities into their classroom and curriculum. When SLIFE feel connected to the content being presented or the skills being taught, they are more likely to engage since it will parallel, or at least tap into, their prior learning experiences (Marshall & DeCapua, 2013; DeCapua & Marshall, 2015).

Discovery Activity: Rethinking the Student-Teacher Relationship

Take a moment and jot down your thoughts on how well you and your students know each other. Here are some questions to consider as you reflect:

- What do you know about them as individuals?
- What do they know about you as a person outside of school?
- What do you know about their families?
- What do they know about your family?
- What do you know about their experiences and lives before they came to your school and you met them in your classroom?

Interconnectedness versus Independence

SLIFE seek personal connections with other members of their class, as well as with their teachers. They need to feel that together they are a community of learners who identify with, support, and aid each other. This feeling of being interconnected to those they are sharing learning experiences with is essential. This second condition of Component A underscores the contrast in how individuals from different cultures view themselves in relation to others in the learning setting. Here again, the difference is a major one, as expressed here:

> I see myself as a member of my group all the time and I have to really be careful with my words and deeds because others see me as their representative.
> —Shirley, Teacher, Chinese-English dual language program

As the discussion of collectivistic cultures in Chapter 1 emphasized, individuals in collectivistic cultures focus on cultivating and deepening relationships, rather than on individual desires and actions and becoming independent. Globally, most cultures are collectivistic (Triandis, 1995); therefore, it is highly likely that SLIFE entering your classrooms will come from a collectivistic culture in which strong and meaningful interpersonal relationships are central.

Interconnectedness is thus for SLIFE a key condition for learning because for them the cornerstone of learning is the unity of people and knowledge. Learning is preferably interpersonal since SLIFE are generally accustomed to learning directly from another person whom they know and with whom they— or someone in their group—has an established relationship. Even in collectivistic cultures characterized by strong status differentiations where teachers are viewed as authority figures, SLIFE often expect to have close relationships with their teachers. These relationships may entail knowing personal information about their teachers, and they may ask questions teachers in formal education would consider inappropriate (DeCapua, 2018; Koch, 2007). Questions like "How many children do you have?" or "Why don't you live with your family?" are not construed by SLIFE as intrusive because they perceive this information as highly important and relevant, and therefore, appropriate to ask a teacher. Questions such as these reflect the collectivistic orientation of many SLIFE, for whom family and familial relations are fundamental (Abi-Hashem, 2018; Segal et al., 2011). While SLIFE may expect to have personal knowledge about their teachers, many SLIFE will still adhere to strong notions of respect for and deferential behavior to the teacher, whom they see as representing authority and knowledge (Flaitz, 2018).

From the earliest school years in formal educational systems as found in, for instance, Canada, Sweden, or the U.S., teachers encourage students to question and explore on their own, including challenging others' opinions, findings, and viewpoints (Keengwe & Onchwari, 2017). As one teacher commented:

> When I make a mistake or offer a biased opinion unapologetically, a good student is not afraid to bring it up and call me on it. I like these types of students even if it means I lose a bit of face. It shows courage, independence, and leadership abilities.
>
> —John, high school social studies teacher

In contrast, SLIFE, who often come from cultures where authority is not questioned and/or where the teacher is of high status, find such behavior threatening to the expected student-teacher social relationship (Ryu & Tuvilla, 2018). SLIFE, used to respecting the status of teachers, may find themselves uncomfortable with teachers such as John, and that discomfort can increase their sense of cultural dissonance. This can be addressed at least partially by teachers promoting a closely-knit learning community in which everyone—the students and teachers—are interconnected in a caring, supportive network of learners who know each other as people.

Interconnectedness is fostered by regular two-way interactions/communication between students and their teachers, as well as among the students themselves, with many opportunities to develop and deepen personal connections during the school day. Students who do not feel connected may disengage (Andrews, 2016; Makarova & Herzog, 2013; Motti-Stefanidi & Masten, 2013). In the younger grades, this type of personal interaction is built into the day, beginning with such common activities as Show and Tell (or Show and Share), in, for instance, Canada, the U.K., and the U.S. In this activity, children recount personal experiences or describe objects meaningful to them during share time. In secondary school, highly personal interaction is expected to occur primarily outside of the classroom, during breaks, lunch, or after school. For SLIFE, regardless of grade or age, social relationships need to be developed inside the classroom and throughout the school community to lessen their sense of cultural dissonance, foster their engagement, and help them develop a comfort level with the school (DeCapua, Marshall & Tang, 2020).

In place of an interpersonal orientation, formal education fosters a gradual separation of people and knowledge. While there are teachers who establish and maintain strong relationships with their students, the primary emphasis of these relationships is to support students in becoming independent learners (Hammond, 2014). In place of an interconnected network of students and teachers that becomes stronger over time, formal education moves in the opposite direction. Over the course of their schooling, students are expected to depend less on each other and on their teachers. Beginning in the earliest school years, students and teachers slowly become more distant, until college, where professors do not necessarily know all their students, particularly in large lecture classes. The focus is on the information, not the student-teacher relationship (Birman & Tran, 2017).

Moreover, popular pedagogical strategies such as differentiated instruction focus on the individual needs, preferences, and abilities of students, with the goal of helping them reach their potential by making them responsible for their learning and building their ability to be independent learners (Meyer et al., 2008). Although group work is often regarded as an important technique, it is not seen as a condition for learning, but rather as a support for learning.

Thinking about our discussion so far, for the next activity, jot down your responses to the questions following these two quotes:

Discovery Activity: What Constitutes Participation?

No matter what I say or what I do, Han and Quozhi don't like to participate in any class activity unless it's small group work.

—Ms. Baldini

My friend know more English so we want help each other.

—Farida, student in Ms. Baldini's class

1. Based on the discussion of conditions for learning, what may be happening in Ms. Baldini's classroom?
2. In what ways are Ms. Baldini's assumptions about learning keeping her from understanding her students better?

These quotes succinctly illustrate a clash between the expectations and preferences of SLIFE and educators. Individual work, participation, and assessment are cornerstones of formal education. Sharing responsibility for learning and accomplishing tasks with those to whom you feel connected dominate in collectivism and informal ways of learning. Ms. Baldini assumes that successful learning and engagement hinge on students' active and individual participation in classroom activities. SLIFE, in contrast, see learning as a collective endeavor in which those who are more knowledgeable mentor those who need support. Students value helping others—at least those with whom they feel interconnected—more than they value completing an assignment on their own.

Table 2.2 Component B: Processes for Learning

SLIFE	Formal Education
Shared Responsibility	Individual Accountability
Oral Transmission	Written Word

Component B: Processes for Learning in Two Settings

Component B focuses on how new material is accessed and transmitted. The two major processes SLIFE are accustomed to in acquiring new knowledge are (1) the sharing of responsibility among a group of learners who rely on one another; and (2) taking in information and ideas in an oral, interactive mode. These two processes, *shared responsibility* and *oral transmission*, contrast directly with the processes used in formal classrooms, namely, *individual accountability* and the *written word*. Students in formal education are individually accountable for their own achievement, and, while the school and the classroom may be viewed as their communities, the focus remains on the needs, abilities, and achievements of individual students (Hanewald, 2013). Additionally, in formal education, the primary means for accessing and disseminating information is print-based. As students move through the grades, curriculum increasingly centers on strong reading and writing skills, so that by the time students are in secondary school, learning primarily takes place through a reliance on their skills in deriving meaning from print-based materials. Table 2.2 illustrates the processes for learning for each of the two contrasting learning paradigms of shared responsibility and individual accountability.

Shared Responsibility versus Individual Accountability

As we saw in the earlier Discovery Activity: *What Constitutes Participation?*, SLIFE come from collectivistic (sub)cultures, with prior learning experiences largely based on informal ways of learning and a focus on mentoring. They tend to prefer learning together and relying on each other to share knowledge and build understanding. They may, in fact, even regard independent learning as selfish (Huang & Lam, 2022).

This perspective directly contrasts with formal education, in which learners seek to show their independence and accept the fact that they will then be individually accountable for their own learning.

This next activity asks you to consider different perspectives. As you respond to the questions, keep in mind your discussion in Discovery Activity, *What Constitutes Participation?*

Discovery Activity: Board Work

Maria stands staring at the board in front of the class and struggles to solve the problem assigned to her by the teacher. Fellow students chime in with suggestions and guidance of all kinds. With their assistance, she is able to complete the problem successfully. Nevertheless, the teacher is disappointed and tells her that it would be so much better if she could do this all by herself without anyone's help.

1. Describe your initial reaction to reading this scenario.
2. How might you explain the students' perspective and the teacher's perspective?
3. Consider what it means to share responsibility and what it means to be individually accountable from the perspective of the SLIFE and of the teacher.

Readers may wish to point out that there is shared learning in formal classrooms—that is, cooperative learning. However, as pointed out in Chapter 1, cultural norms influence how people view collaboration and how they participate in cooperative learning activities (Huma, 2016). Group learning is centered around each student ultimately being given a specific job that they must be accountable for (Johnson & Johnson, 2017). Take, for example, the popular cooperative activity, Jigsaw (https://www.jigsaw.org). In this activity, each member of the group is assigned one part of a learning task or problem and becomes an "expert" in that area. In larger classes, group members join with members of other groups with the same assignment to research and/ or share ideas. After students have worked on their assignments, they rejoin their original groups to present their findings and to "piece together" a clear understanding of the learning task or problem. Each person's piece of the puzzle combines to form a completed jigsaw of knowledge; the students must rely on each other's expertise to obtain the necessary information to complete the group's learning task or problem. While there is group learning and group responsibility in the jigsaw activity, "students then apply their knowledge to a group task or to an individual task, assuring individual accountability for all information" (Peregoy & Boyle, 2022, p. 93).

As illustrated by the jigsaw activity, cooperative learning in formal education is conducted as a team with each member responsible and accountable for a particular task or assignment to complete. For people from collectivistic cultures who have had minimal exposure to formal education, group work is enacted more as an ensemble (Mejía-Arauz et al., 2018). By extension, most SLIFE view learning as something that is accomplished cooperatively. The knowledge load is shared; they see themselves as a group of learners working together to construct knowledge. If we think of an orchestra, we think of the many players and instruments playing different notes, entering and ending at different times, yet the contributions of all the players playing together is what creates the music.

Oral Transmission versus the Written Word

In formal education, reading and writing skills are among the key criteria by which SLIFE are defined, that is, they are evaluated based on how well they read and write, either in their home language or in English. In terms of the learning paradigm perspective we are using, engaging in print-based literacy practices is a key process for learning. Yet for SLIFE, their world is primarily, if not exclusively, one of orality. They come with a strong tradition of learning through oral transmission.

Some SLIFE come from cultures with little or no written language; others come from cultures with strong written traditions but have not had opportunities to develop strong reading and writing skills in any language. This is a major difference among SLIFE. One further distinction between groups who rely on oral and other modes of communication, both verbal and nonverbal, versus those who rely on written communication, is whether or not related self-esteem issues develop.

In societies where orality is primary, lack of literacy skills does not signal a deficiency and therefore does not result in self-esteem issues. Many of the languages in the world have no written form or have only recently developed one. These languages include many of the Indigenous languages of peoples of Asia, Africa, and the Americas. Print-based literacy has not been central in these cultures or subcultures. Knowledge, history, stories, values, beliefs and religious and cultural practices are all preserved and transmitted orally, and elders, who are regarded as keepers of this collective knowledge, may not practice literacy at all (Watson, 2019).

On the other hand, in societies where print-based literacy plays a major role, many are disenfranchised from participating in education to develop reading and writing skills, usually a result of poverty and the lack of access to schools. Those members are frequently stigmatized, face limited opportunities, and frequently have self-esteem issues (Floyd & Sakellariou, 2017).

Table 2.3 Typical Literacy Backgrounds of SLIFE

Preliterate	Students have had no prior exposure to reading and writing; students' home languages may not be written, be recently written, and/or there may be few written materials available in the home languages.
Nonliterate	Students' home languages have a written form, but students have not had access to instruction in reading and writing.
Semiliterate:	Students have basic reading and writing skills but not enough to participate fully in grade-level schooling.

(DeCapua, Marshall & Tang, 2020, p. 40)

Other SLIFE may be speakers of a language different from the majority language of their home country. The language they speak may not have a written form, may not be valued enough to be taught, and/or may have few print materials. Such SLIFE have had unequal access to developing reading and writing skills since the majority language, which is generally also the language of schooling, is not their language. Because these students may have been introduced to but have not mastered basic print-based skills, they therefore continue to face significant issues, including being able to further their education and access to better paid jobs (Kaiper-Marquez, 2020). Table 2.3 briefly summarizes reading and writing backgrounds.

As we see, SLIFE come to formal education in their new country with a range of print-based literacy backgrounds. Despite these differences in their experiences with reading and writing, all SLIFE share the perspective that oral transmission, not the written word, is primary in their lives. They do not turn to print materials as a resource for information or for developing their knowledge. Reading and writing have not played important roles in their lives, nor have their prior literacy practices encouraged them to acquire and exchange knowledge from print sources. Print-based literacy, if it exists for their cultural group, is often restricted to a few adults, usually males, who function as de facto scribes for others (Whitescarver & Kalman, 2009).

SLIFE with basic reading and writing skills frequently view print-based materials as purely utilitarian sources. For instance, reading can serve very specific and limited roles, such as reading a fast-food menu, deciphering utility bills, or engaging with social media (Hoffman, 2019). When they do use print-based sources, they must be contextualized and meaningful. They must be "brought to life" through extensive discussions among the reader(s) and the audience. Such discussions contextualize the impersonal text by supplying extensive background, for example, a description of how a particular dispute started, an examination of how the members involved are related, or the recounting of stories perhaps only tangentially related to the text (Salomon & Apaza, 2006). The text is secondary to oral communication.

Even storytelling, found in all cultures, is notably different between oral and written modes, demonstrating clearly the difference in conventions between oral communication and print. Print-based narrative storytelling uses a literary register without sustained efforts to "mimic orality through diction, syntax, or other devices of linguistic discourse" (Fagundes, 2007, p.138). Such narrative storytelling contrasts with oral storytelling, which uses and mimics the actual speech of characters by including representative syntax, accent, and vocabulary that "point to the world of primary orality" (p. 138). Oral transmission requires redundancy and repetition, and poetic devices used to facilitate memorization, all of which provide rhythm and make it easier to remember.

Formal education is based on the assumption that students will engage in continual, print-based textual interaction with content-area knowledge. A parallel assumption is that textual engagement increases in complexity as students progress through the grades (Cavallaro & Sembiante, 2020). From the earliest grades onward, teachers and students together build and create meaning with print. Children learn that reading and writing are interactive processes, where readers and writers consider what meaning is and how meaning is conveyed (Frankel et al., 2017). As they develop their reading skills, children also develop important metacognitive skills such as monitoring, checking, and amending their reading processes. In learning to write, children learn to organize and express their ideas in a variety of ways by practicing creating their own texts—whether functional, creative, or other—for different audiences.

Moreover, formal education is based on an evolving dependence on the written word for the retention and mastery of subject matter. Based on the belief that print-based literacy development begins early in life and is ongoing, educators and psychologists advocate reading to children, providing an environment rich in print-based materials and activities, and nurturing children's desire to read through the use of specific reading practices beginning early in childhood (Bower, 2014). Through the written word, which includes the internet, people have immediate access to infinitely more information than any one person could possibly retain.

The difference in perspective on the written word between those who have fully participated in formal education and SLIFE is another factor leading to the sense of cultural dissonance felt by the latter. SLIFE have difficulty making the transition from oral transmission to accessing new information from print-based materials, as, for example, in following directions from textbooks and using books to learn. These students, even after they have learned to read, often turn to someone else to explain meaning to them because they continue to experience difficulties extracting meaning from print (DeCapua, Marshall &

Tang, 2020). In one science class, for example, we observed how the teacher carefully reviewed the instructions for an upcoming activity. Yet, once she had released students to work in their groups, the SLIFE kept asking her to tell them again what to do, even when she went over and pointed to the instructions and re-read them with each group.

Component C: Activities for Learning in Two Settings

Finally, we come to the largest overall difference between SLIFE prior learning experiences and formal education—the cognitive processes and types of activities required of learners. Just as we have seen the contrast between the conditions and processes for learning, we now examine the mismatch between the types of activities SLIFE are used to doing, and the types of common classroom learning activities and associated ways of thinking. While in both paradigms learners engage in activities that further their knowledge and mastery of skills, the associated cognitive processes entailed in formal education differ greatly from those in informal ways of learning.

Activities, as a learning paradigm component, is a general or broad term encompassing a variety of tasks that are performed by the learner to build ability and subsequently master. Cooking, childcare, artisanal skills, shepherding, farming, and construction work are examples of the types of pragmatic activities familiar to many SLIFE. The pragmatic tasks they perform in service of these activities have concrete, utilitarian results. Because SLIFE have primarily experienced learning in the context of real-world activities, they are accustomed to executing the types of tasks that directly result in the successful performance of those "lived experiences."

Such learning consists of sociocultural experiences that are age-appropriate and that draw on community-shared skills and knowledge, or funds of knowledge. While there is no formal curriculum, there is a road map to follow in determining the content that will be covered over time, such as through an apprenticeship model, consisting of observation, imitation, practice, feedback, more advanced practice, additional feedback, and ultimately, success. Another way skills and knowledge are built is through ongoing mutual engagement in practices in which younger members are increasingly given greater responsibilities over time as they participate in significant community and family rituals, ceremonies, and enterprises (Mejía-Arauz et al., 2018). The activities for learning are contextualized throughout and the learner sees how the practice relates directly to the subsequent accomplishment of the overall task at hand. Making soup, for example, is a pragmatic activity that entails such tasks as peeling vegetables, slicing them, and adding water. The end result will be a meal that satisfies a practical need for nourishment.

Table 2.4 Component C: Activities for Learning

SLIFE	Formal Education
Pragmatic Tasks	Decontextualized Tasks
based on lived experiences	based on academic ways of thinking

In contrast, formal education demands that SLIFE perform school-based activities, many of which include a variety of decontextualized tasks, such as completing graphic organizers, tables, or charts, distinguishing between fact and fiction, or organizing and sequencing information in paragraphs and essays. These tasks require (and build) specific associated cognitive processes, i.e., academic ways of thinking, such as defining, categorizing and classifying, and synthesizing, to develop understanding and build content knowledge. These are ways of thinking grounded in logical modes of reasoning based on observable facts, are found in all disciplines and are the cornerstones of formal education. For example, the task of filling out a graphic organizer may require categorizing, determining cause and effect, or comparing and contrasting. These academic ways of thinking are represented in Bloom's Taxonomy (1956) and Anderson et al., (2001). (See DeCapua, Marshall & Tang, (2020) for a more extensive discussion and examples.)

Component C: Activities for Learning comprises these two aspects, i.e., the tasks themselves and the underlying foundation for them. Table 2.4 illustrates the elements of this component for each of the two learning paradigms: Pragmatic tasks based on lived experiences and decontextualized tasks based on academic ways of thinking.

When formal education is not present, oral traditions are especially important in transmitting knowledge and skills from adults to children (Watson, 2019). SLIFE generally learn by doing, following a role model, operating within a context, and obtaining feedback from the results themselves or from other people in their community (Paradise & Rogoff, 2009; Rogoff, 2014). The key activity is practice, preceded by observation and followed by monitoring. Generally speaking, pragmatic activities occur within a context and have some real-world application that is immediately apparent. They are based on the lived experiences of the members of a social community.

Memorization and rote learning with little or even no reference to or reliance on print, are often major strengths SLIFE bring with them as a result of their experiences with oral transmission, have little place in formal education today. Their rhetorical skills get them only so far, as the focus on academic activities requires that they use their knowledge in service of critical thinking rather than to accomplish a real-world task. In social studies and history courses, students are asked to define terms and to analyze and interpret primary and secondary sources; in math they are expected to make logical deductions; in English language arts they relate themes in literature to life and are expected to identify and explain different genres; and in science they must know the scientific method. These activities are neither intrinsically natural nor necessary for learning, but they are the way people are expected to learn in formal educational settings. Muhammed, for example, had attended a Qur'an school, was literate in Arabic, and could read religious passages and recite them from memory. On the other hand, he had little subject area content knowledge and was not used to engaging in academic ways of thinking, such as comparing and contrasting or classification.

What we are referring to as academic activities, on the other hand, are decontextualized school-based tasks designed for the purpose of developing and applying concepts that are not integral aspects of students' or teachers' lived experiences, but rather are part of the general canon of the knowledge base of formal education. These tasks are grounded in literacy and require associated academic ways of thinking. We define *decontextualization* as "the handling of information in a way that either disconnects other information or backgrounds it" (Denny, 1991, p. 66). In using the term decontextualized, we are referring to the absence of a real-world situation that is immediately relevant to the lives of students, in which to place the learning activity. Related to the concept of decontextualization is how information is presented in formal education. Specifically, how is academic knowledge separate from pragmatic knowledge? In Chapter 1, for instance, we saw the question, "What do dogs and rabbits have in common?" We noted how this question would be answered differently, depending on a person's degree of participation in formal education.

Luria (1979) investigated preliterate farmers in a region of the former Soviet Union who had not been exposed to formal education. He showed the farmers four pictures: an ax, a hammer, a log, and a saw, and asked them to pick the one item they thought did not belong with the others. In this research, which has subsequently been replicated by many others across the world, Luria found that the farmers uniformly discarded one of the tools, usually the hammer, because for them, only the log provided a meaningful context, that of using the remaining tools to do something with the log. Here we see the influence of relying only on lived experiences when confronting a task, even one that is clearly hypothetical in nature. Most people with formal education, in contrast, discard the log because the hammer, ax, and saw can all be categorized as tools. As shown in Chapter 1, categorization, based on abstract concepts, is an essential feature of formal education.

As we have described elsewhere, decontextualized school-based tasks and associated ways of thinking form a hidden challenge (DeCapua, 2019; DeCapua, Marshall & Tang, 2020; DeCapua & Triulzi, 2020; Marshall & DeCapua, 2013). Beyond the earliest years of primary school, teachers in formal education expect that students will know how to perform tasks that require academic ways of thinking. Yet for SLIFE, task-based learning activities constitute a "curriculum" they must learn, along with their new language and subject matter. SLIFE face a major hurdle in learning not only how to perform academic tasks, but how to change the way they think about the world in order to reposition themselves to succeed with such tasks.

Two Learning Paradigms

Table 2.5 summarizes the three components of learning paradigms—that of SLIFE and that of formal education—discussed in this chapter: conditions for learning, processes for learning, and activities for learning. For each, we see that the items on the left (SLIFE) are in direct contrast to those on the right (formal education).

Because SLIFE have had limited or no exposure to formal education, they have a limited conceptual understanding of such a learning paradigm. Their paradigm and ours conflict with each other, another factor in creating the sense of cultural dissonance SLIFE experience. Instead of immediate relevance and interconnectedness, SLIFE find that formal education is future-oriented and promotes independent learning. In place of their familiar learning processes of shared responsibility and oral transmission, SLIFE are confronted with the expectation of individual accountability and learning primarily from the written word. Finally, SLIFE, who are accustomed to pragmatic tasks, encounter decontextualized tasks and ways of thinking that do not match their experience.

Table 2.5 Two Different Learning Paradigms

SLIFE	Formal Education
Conditions for Learning	
Immediate relevance	Future relevance
Interconnectedness	Independence
Processes for Learning	
Shared responsibility	Individual accountability
Oral transmission	Written word
Activities for Learning	
Pragmatic tasks based on lived experiences	Decontextualized tasks based on academic ways of thinking

For Further Exploration

1. Return to what you jotted down in the two Discovery Activities *What is Relevance?* (page 36) and *Rethinking the Student-Teacher Relationship* (page 37).

   a. After reading this chapter how much would you say your thoughts reflect those of formal education? Explain.

   b. How might you describe the relationship between culture, learning, and teaching based on these two Discovery Activities?

2. Consider this perspective from Justin, a high school student:

   I hate group work. The teacher is always assigning me to a group where I end up doing all the work. I only want to do my share. If the others don't do their share, we all get a bad grade. So, I just told the teacher "I did my share."

   a. How does Justin navigate the space between shared responsibility and individual accountability?

   b. How do you think SLIFE might approach the same type of activity?

3. In his ESL class, Mr. Aguero invited students to provide midpoint feedback on his teaching, so that he could adjust as needed for the remainder of the course. He asked each student to highlight what they liked best about the classes. Most responded with specific activities, such as class discussions, or word analyses for vocabulary expansion. Koua, the only Hmong student, instead reacted by saying "I like that we all work together to help each other learn."

   a. Looking back at Question 2, reread Justin's comments and think about how they contrast with Koua's view.

   b. How do these two diverging views, that of Justin and Koua, cause you to reconsider your approach to group work for both types of students?

4. Mrs. Zukowski is working with her SLIFE on geometric shapes. After reviewing them, she gives each student a bag of geometric shapes. Each shape comes in a variety of colors. She tells them to take these items out of the bag, sort them by shape, and then put all the squares, rectangles, etc., in the appropriately labeled boxes, on a desk. After a few minutes, Mrs. Zukowski sees that the students are confused and she realizes that they don't understand how to group by shape when the shapes are different colors. For them, a red circle and a blue circle don't belong together, but a blue circle, blue triangle, and blue octagon do belong together. Based on

the discussion in this chapter, how would you explain the difficulty the students are having?

5. This vignette allows a glimpse into a student who faced major difficulties upon entering school in the United States and eventually dropped out:

> Hayder, a Kurdish refugee, entered high school with second grade reading and writing skills. He attended school but never completed homework assignments. However, outside of class Hayder "would read billboards while driving, signs on buildings, instructions and messages at an ATM, and messages and directions while playing video games" (Sarroub, Pernicek, & Sweeney, 2007, p. 676).

a. How do you see this anecdote relating to the notion of immediate, practical relevance?

b. How might Hayder's teachers have built on what he did like to read to motivate and engage him?

3. An Introduction to MALP: The Mutually Adaptive Learning Paradigm

> "Teachers feel that students walk into their universe, and that they must do as the teacher says, forgetting that not everyone has had the same experiences."
>
> —Leslie

Focusing primarily or even exclusively on aspects of language, approaches to learning, or what teachers need to do to facilitate learning, is just the beginning of our broader task in this book. The general inflexibility of the structures embedded in formal education can hinder the transition of students such as SLIFE to academic achievement and social integration (Koehler & Schneider, 2019; Menken, 2010), regardless of their teachers' efforts, however well-intentioned. One solution might be to teach SLIFE according to the conditions, processes, and activities of their own learning paradigm. In this way, SLIFE might feel more comfortable and more receptive to learning. However, few will succeed in moving through the grades, in passing the standardized assessments, or in contemporary society in general with this approach, as it does not include mastery of print literacy or the activities for learning in formal educational settings. A second alternative is to teach according to the learning paradigm of formal education and expect SLIFE to grasp it in its entirety as they move through the system. Unfortunately, this plan also results in failure, as they cannot catch on and catch up due to the significant challenges and cultural dissonance they are experiencing.

The question then arises: What can teachers do? Given the major differences we have seen between the learning paradigm of SLIFE and the learning paradigm of formal education, it is clear that what is needed is a new learning paradigm to assist this population in succeeding in our educational system. We argue, therefore, that we need a learning paradigm based on an instructional approach that offers a mutually adaptive mindset. Such an approach neither requires teachers to make a complete shift to the learner's paradigm, nor forces students to make an immediate and complete shift to the learning paradigm of formal education. Here we explore in depth what this approach is and how it is implemented.

Addressing Cultural Dissonance

In Chapters 1 and 2, we examined the worldview of SLIFE and how it causes them to see the roles of teachers and learners through the lenses of orality, collectivism, and informal ways of learning. This worldview, in turn, creates major cultural dissonance for them in school. In this chapter, we begin by presenting a framework to address this dissonance.

Intercultural Communication Framework

We propose three principles designed to create a classroom as community, to intentionally build in culturally responsive and sustaining pedagogy, and to increase communication and understanding. These principles form the basis of our Intercultural Communication Framework and underlie our instructional approach, the Mutually Adaptive Learning Paradigm (DeCapua, Marshall & Tang, 2020; Marshall, 1998; Marshall & DeCapua, 2013).

The Intercultural Communication Framework
1. Establish and maintain ongoing two-way communication.
2. Identify priorities in our culture and our students' cultures.
3. Build associations between the familiar and unfamiliar.

Principle 1: Establish and Maintain Ongoing Two-Way Communication

The tendency for schools is to set up communication between school and home in which the role of the school is to inform students and their families. Such communication ranges from providing students and families with materials on school policies and/or government regulations to having meetings with an interpreter present. These initiatives are an important part of the school-family relationship, yet they are strictly one-way communication with a focus on conveying information rather than on obtaining it. Communication should also flow in the other direction, so that school staff and teachers can listen to and learn from students' families (Fruja & Roxas, 2016; Madziva & Thondhlana, 2017). While some families may feel uncomfortable communicating with the school, they will be more willing to share information and viewpoints if family members are approached in a warm and friendly manner and with general rather than specific questions. SLIFE and their families have a great deal of information to impart to school personnel about their backgrounds, their needs, their perspectives, and how they view the school experience (Croce, 2018). This knowledge will help classroom teachers to understand their students better and not simply to see them as SLIFE who are confronting numerous challenges in school, but rather as individuals who have valuable prior experiences and outside responsibilities, whether working, taking care of other family members, or living alone as heads of households (Hos, 2020).

When communication occurs in both directions, there is more opportunity to reduce cultural dissonance for SLIFE. Once such communication has been established, teachers can obtain, and subsequently leverage, a great deal of knowledge that will assist in following the remaining two principles: Principle 2, Identify and Accommodate Priorities; and Principle 3, Build Associations Between Familiar and Unfamiliar concepts.

The scene described in the box, from Lewis Carroll's *Alice in Wonderland*, illustrates the importance of this first principle.

Discovery Activity: Explain Yourself

In *Alice's Adventures in Wonderland* by Lewis Carroll, Alice encounters a very strange and peculiar world where animals and playing cards talk. After an incident in which Alice shrinks to a very small size and is wandering around among blades of grass, she encounters a mushroom about her height with a caterpillar sitting on top. When the caterpillar notices Alice, he asks, "Who are you?" and wants Alice to explain herself to him. She tells him that this is rather difficult because when she got up this morning, she knew who she was, yet strange events had been happening to her and she is now rather confused as to who she is. As Alice tries to explain her confusion to the caterpillar, he finds Alice's confusion strange and asks her again to explain who she is. Yet, when Alice asks the caterpillar who *he* is, he asks her why he should need to explain who he is.

1. How does this excerpt relate to the cultural dissonance addressed in this text? Consider how Alice's sense of reality has changed.
2. Explain how you can relate this excerpt to the idea of needing to establish and maintain communication with SLIFE.

Figure 3.1. Alice and the Caterpillar

Principle 2: Identify and Accommodate Priorities

Discovery Activity: School Priorities

1. Jot down four to six behaviors, expectations, and routines and/or procedures that you believe are priorities in school, in the classroom, and in learning.
2. Based on what you have learned so far about SLIFE, which of the items you listed might result in a clash of priorities and cause discomfort for this population? Explain.
3. How might you determine whether to accommodate the SLIFE priority or to assert your own? Justify your response.

The second principle of the Intercultural Communication Framework is that of identifying priorities. This can be challenging because people are generally unaware of their own cultural priorities, which are part of the subconscious knowledge they have by virtue of membership in that culture (DeCapua, 2018). As we explored in Chapters 1 and 2, teachers and mainstream students in formal educational systems as found for instance, in Australia, Canada, the U.K., and the U.S., share a set of assumptions that can be seen as priorities for school.

School priorities consist of what is most important to teachers and/ or students, and what must be in place for a successful teaching or learning experience. For example, in formal classrooms, students are expected to be individually responsible for class or homework assignments unless the teacher specifically indicates otherwise. This is a priority because it provides teachers with essential information on each student's grasp of the material, so that ultimately each student can receive the best instruction and a fair assessment in the form of a grade.

SLIFE have their own assumptions about learning that exemplify their cultural priorities that do not match those of formal education. For one, SLIFE generally believe that feelings of interconnectedness with fellow students and with the teacher are more important than being independent learners. Working together to share responsibility is a priority because it fosters their sense of community and helps to recreate their familiar learning paradigm.

Regular school attendance, on the other hand, is not a priority for most SLIFE. Pastoor (2015) describes how Karin, a teacher in Norway, was having difficulty with two SLIFE who were not attending class. In formal education systems, students are expected to be present and on time a set number of days each week for the entire school year, except for designated holidays or for very specific types of absences. As a teacher, Karin's priority was regular attendance. For her students, who were recently-arrived Afghan refugees, attendance was based on how they felt that day, not on any sense of obligation. They also did not share the concept of regularity and routine, which was not surprising given the disruptions they had faced in their lives.

Cultural dissonance is exacerbated when these assumptions are not brought to the level of conscious awareness and dealt with in a culturally responsive manner. Previously, you read how Janice's high school students struggled with what to do with lined paper. To address Principle 2, teachers must continually differentiate between what is important and what is a minor detail in each and every situation. This may seem like an obvious teaching strategy, since much of teaching focuses on identifying and conveying what is important. The difference, however, is that as teachers of SLIFE, we cannot lose sight of the fact that these students come, for the most part, from cultures with vastly different learning paradigms and different formal schemata.

What SLIFE may consider important or essential information may be overlooked, ignored, or considered minor, from the formal academic point of view. The key point here is that when a priority for SLIFE can be accommodated, even if it differs from your priorities as a teacher, it should be. One example is the need for immediate relevance. If SLIFE feel they cannot learn unless they see a connection to their lives, then you can accommodate that priority by, for instance, introducing new content by finding something relevant to their daily lives first, and then bringing in the content. Seek to include elements of students' pragmatic knowledge and bring in content that incorporates a connection to their lives. To do so, however, teachers need to be sure they have been following—and continue to follow—Principle 1, Establish and Maintain Ongoing Two-Way Communication.

At the same time, when SLIFE must honor a new classroom priority, they will need to adapt. Although most SLIFE do not share print as a priority, you as their teacher will insist that the development of strong reading and writing skills, and the ability to use these skills to access information, is a priority in this new classroom setting. While in the past SLIFE have gained knowledge and skills and shared information through oral transmission, they will now need to prioritize print-based literacy to succeed in school.

Regular attendance is another new priority SLIFE will need to consider. Returning to Karin and her Afghan students, she negotiated a coping strategy with them about how to handle coming to school. They agreed together that they would not decide about coming to school until they had gotten up and were ready to go. If they still did not feel like they could come to school, they would text Karin and let her know. Here is the exchange:

So we made a deal, a joint agreement that they should not decide that they were ill before they got up, had taken a shower and eaten breakfast, unless they actually had a fever.

Interviewer: Did it work?

Karin: Yes, he is at school much more [laughs], and the same applies to this girl. It was rather sweet, one of the first times she did not come to school I got a text message: 'I have done everything you said Karin but I am still not able to come to school.'

(Pastoor, 2015, p. 249)

This give and take, or mutual adaptation, demonstrates a willingness on your part to take into account learner priorities, while at the same time ensuring that crucial priorities of learner success, such as individual accountability, print-based literacy, and academic ways of thinking, are encouraged.

To be effective in introducing new priorities, teachers will need to use Principle 3, Build Associations Between Familiar and Unfamiliar Concepts.

Discovery Activity: A Different Lens

Recall in Chapter 1 the Discovery Activity *No Pencils, No Books* (see page 21). Remember that you were asked to imagine being at a professional development meeting where there was no access to print or recording materials of any type.

1. As highly educated people with a strong reliance on print-based literacy, make a list of three to five strategies that would build bridges between the familiar (the written word) and the unfamiliar (exclusive oral transmission) to help you cope in a situation like this.
2. Now, using your knowledge of SLIFE, what might their strategies be, given their strengths and cultural characteristics as outlined in previous chapters?
3. Which of these strategies would also work for you? Which would not? Explain your response.

Principle 3: Build Associations Between Familiar and Unfamiliar Concepts

The third principle asks for teachers to build associations between the familiar and the new. Activating prior knowledge is one of the most important strategies in helping all students learn. To do so requires that we continue following Principle 1. When working with SLIFE, we want to keep in mind that although these students may not have grade-level academic knowledge, they come to the class with substantial real-world experiential knowledge. When we can relate the knowledge and experiences of these students to the curriculum content, doing so forms a bridge between familiar and unfamiliar material. Beth Ann described, for instance, how her Haitian SLIFE during a lab on sound were able to draw on their personal knowledge to explain how drums worked, despite their low proficiency in English.

One instructor was struggling to have students grasp the concept of clip art and line drawings as two-dimensional depictions of three-dimensional reality. The instructor asked the students to draw objects in the classroom and show them to each other for labeling and identification. In this way, students began to see the relationship between the three-dimensional world they were familiar with, and the new two-dimensional view. This, in turn, led to a better grasp of the schematics and diagrams so often used in classrooms that are so unfamiliar to most SLIFE.

Taken together, these three principles—of establishing and maintaining communication, identifying and accommodating priorities, and building associations—function to address and reduce the cultural dissonance of SLIFE, by helping them transition to the learning paradigm of formal education. Teachers who infuse these principles into the daily work of teaching and interacting with SLIFE and their families will be taking a major step toward improving the school experience of these students.

Culturally Responsive and Sustaining Teaching

Geneva Gay (2000; 2018), building and expanding on earlier work by Ladson-Billings (1995), has been instrumental in fostering culturally responsive teaching. The basic premise is that mainstream middle-class values and expectations are privileged while those of other culturally and linguistically diverse populations are overlooked, devalued, and excluded. In not recognizing or acknowledging what these other student populations bring to the educational experience, educators are taking a deficit view focused on what these students lack (Nieto & Bode, 2018; Snyder & Fenner, 2021).

In our work on SLIFE, Gay's research in culturally responsive teaching has guided us in providing a template for addressing the principles we have explored in the Intercultural Communication Framework (ICF). Her five basic precepts are (1) cultural competence, (2) a culturally relevant curriculum, (3) a supportive learning community, (4) cultural congruity; and (5) effective instruction. As we examine Gay's five precepts of culturally responsive teaching through a SLIFE lens, we can see how accepted best practices must be reconceptualized to be effective for them.

First, *cultural competence* demands that educators develop a deep awareness of who their students are, their cultural backgrounds, and their prior learning experiences. This entails going well beyond a surface level of awareness based on typical foods, clothing, and music, to cultivating a continually expanding knowledge base about the deeper aspects of SLIFE cultures (DeCapua & Marshall, 2015; DeCapua & Wintergerst, 2016; Ngo, 2010). As an example, one high school was receiving a sizable number of Guatemalan students, many of whom were being screened, identified, and then assessed as SLIFE. However, what the school did not at first realize was that these students were Indigenous

Maya K'iche' with their own distinctive language and culture. Their culture was not the blend of Spanish and Mayan influences commonly associated with Guatemala, but rather a traditional Mayan culture with centuries of oral tradition rooted in a strong collectivistic worldview. Without awareness of this key cultural information, the teachers would not have been as prepared to work with this subpopulation of students.

For the second precept, a *culturally relevant curriculum,* teachers use their evolving cultural competence to build curricula consistently infused with cultural elements and content that is meaningful to students. Key is the "funds of knowledge" approach proposed by González, Moll & Amanti (2005), Moll & Greenberg (1990), and Moll et al., (1992), in which the large stores of knowledge culturally and linguistically diverse learners bring to the classroom, although outside the traditional canon of formal educational knowledge, are actively explored and incorporated into the classroom. Carol, for instance, before introducing the nineteenth century U.S. president Abraham Lincoln and his efforts to end slavery, had the students engage in a WebQuest on a famous person from their own country. For this project, one of the K'iche' students learned about Tecum Uman, a major K'iche' hero who is honored by a well-known statue in his community.

Third, a *supportive learning community* is what we as teachers in general strive to foster; however, from the perspective of culturally responsive and sustaining instruction, this means knowing which cultural differences are likely to affect student behavior. For example, if students are not comfortable with looking someone in a position of authority in the eye, teachers may evaluate this reluctance as inattention or disrespect. In addition, in a supportive learning community, the languages, the knowledge, the skills, and the abilities of SLIFE are valued, respected, and fostered. In the case of K'iche' students, for example, speakers are accustomed to their language and culture being viewed negatively, as is true for many Indigenous peoples in Latin America. Such prejudice may affect their willingness to communicate in their home language or even acknowledge that it is their dominant or preferred language.

The fourth precept, *cultural congruity,* requires teachers to understand that there are different ways of teaching and learning, and to actively promote them in their classrooms. Since cultural differences in socialization practices result in different cognitive pathways (Cole, 2005; Rogoff, 2014), teachers cannot assume that commonly accepted best pedagogical practices will meet the needs of SLIFE whose ways of learning and processing information are frequently different from those of their peers with age-appropriate formal education. This precept, in particular, undergirds much of our instructional approach, as will be seen later on in this chapter.

And finally, *effective instruction* means that teaching SLIFE takes neither a deficit perspective nor a remedial stance. For SLIFE, reading and writing skills, grade-level content, decontextualized tasks, and associated academic ways of thinking, are new and must be introduced, carefully scaffolded, and practiced as such. This requires incorporating all the knowledge and skills from the first four precepts and operationalizing them in the classroom.

Discovery Activity: Holiday Gift Giving

The Christmas holiday was approaching and Mr. Spencer was working with his adult class of SLIFE, all Christian, studying in a community-based English program. He decided to combine a unit on budgets and purchases with holiday gifts for friends and family. He brought in advertisements from local stores and shared websites with special deals, selecting those that were in the immediate area and that students would be likely to go to for their purchases.

The students resisted the activity and stared at him, wondering why they were asked to engage in the task of finding what they might buy as gifts. After much consternation on both sides, the teacher and his class brought to the surface the cultural assumptions that made this activity not a culturally responsive one for this group of students.

These students, financially struggling refugees and immigrants, saw exchanging Christmas gifts as wasteful; instead, they bought only what they needed, and if they did give something to another person, friend or family, they chose something utilitarian. Any extra money they had, they remitted to their families back home. So, the idea of an "extra" item bought for Christmas was not something they related to at all, particularly since this was for them primarily a religious holiday.

1. How does this classroom conflict relate to Gay's precepts of cultural responsiveness?
2. What could Mr. Spencer have done to avoid this misunderstanding?
3. What other type of activity could he create for his work on budgets and purchases that would respond to their cultural norms?

Recently, the commitment to sustaining, not only being responsive to, the languages and cultures of culturally and linguistically diverse students has become central in education (Paris & Alim, 2017). Teachers actively incorporate student knowledge, experiences, and skills; they learn from their students, identify with them as learners and as people with extensive funds of knowledge, and plan and revisit lessons accordingly. The role of the teacher becomes both that of teacher and learner, based on relationships and interactions deriving from these relationships. Teachers intentionally commit to providing the means for student voices and choices to be a part of the instructional conversation, in ways that embrace and validate them in their own right and not only as a means to an end (Paris & Alim, 2014).

Implementing culturally responsive and sustaining education conforms to our book's premise that we are *breaking new ground* for SLIFE and focusing on *creating fertile spaces* for teaching and learning, rather than filling in gaps in their learning. We believe that by thinking of ourselves as gardeners, and seeing our job as cultivating the ground that best nurtures our students, we can enable them to reach their full potential (Robinson, 2006).

Pamela Broussard, founder of the Leading ELLs! website, also speaks of learning as it applies to SLIFE in terms of gardening. She describes how initially she had tried gathering wild sunflowers and growing them at home. Although she provided nutrients and sufficient sun and water, they failed to thrive in their new home. In querying more experienced gardeners, she learned that it was essential to use wildflowers' original soil whenever transplanting them. SLIFE, like the sunflowers, have been uprooted from their natural environment. Unless we as educators keep some of their "original soil," that is, acknowledging and building on what SLIFE bring with them, they will not respond or thrive even when other aspects of their educational environment are optimal (Broussard, 2020). One of the major conditions for the success of SLIFE entails deliberately incorporating their languages and cultural backgrounds in as many ways as possible when introducing new learning experiences.

One important asset SLIFE bring to our classrooms is their oral skills. Because reading and writing are not central to their lives, they have developed strong oral skills, often even in more than one language or dialect. Their oral strengths are rooted in their original soil, strengths that we can leverage in our classrooms by allowing and promoting *translanguaging*. In the monolingual approach to language learning, learners are expected, if not required, to use only the target language to engage in activities, negotiate meaning, and to communicate. In translanguaging, in contrast, the whole linguistic repertoire of each learner, in any and all languages (or dialects), regardless of proficiency, are considered equally valid and regarded as invaluable assets in scaffolding learning (Garcia & Wei, 2014). By fostering translanguaging, we encourage SLIFE to use their considerable oral skills to develop and build metalinguistic and metacognitive skills, in addition to their reading and writing abilities, to access new knowledge and content in English, in order to thrive in our classrooms.

By intentionally leveraging the oral skills of SLIFE, teachers also maintain cultural elements important to the students. If we look at culture more broadly, rather than as specific to one ethnicity or nationality, we can see patterns across these groups that lead us to understand how they may share some values and traditions which distinguish them from those associated with formal education. Watson (2019) has identified key shared values and practices among oral cultures that transcend any one particular ethnicity or nationality. One critical area she examines is the often-overlooked oral skills and preference for orality in many cultures represented by SLIFE. The intentional incorporation into our teaching of the oral assets SLIFE bring with them is a means of providing equity and inclusion, as well as honoring, validating, and sustaining what is culturally familiar to them. For example, Bigelow & Vinogradov, (2011), and Perry (2008) describe how teachers successfully leveraged cultural storytelling practices to develop both reading and writing skills and English language proficiency among SLIFE with minimal or no literacy skills in any language. Playsted (2018) recounts how she used singing in her teaching of Yazidi refugees who had very little written language but had a robust tradition of passing down knowledge through hymns. These examples of teachers purposefully interweaving valued and familiar oral cultural practices of their students into their pedagogy, illustrate what Watson calls *transculturing* (Watson, 2019, p.5). Much like translanguaging, it allows all students to access familiar pathways, in this case their oral assets, as they navigate learning in formal settings. The incorporation of transculturing in designing instruction for SLIFE can be a powerful way of implementing culturally sustaining pedagogy. Part Two of this book presents projects that leverage the oral strengths of SLIFE.

In developing an approach to working with SLIFE and maximizing their potential, we have taken into account the culturally responsive and sustaining pedagogical perspective and created what we have termed a "mutually adaptive" learning paradigm that both honors and validates the home and preferred languages and cultures of students, while at the same time it explicitly focuses on the processes and activities for learning required for success in formal education. It is to this new paradigm for learning that we now turn our attention.

The Mutually Adaptive Learning Paradigm

Culturally responsive pedagogy focuses on accommodating and responding to students' academic, cultural, linguistic, and social needs through teaching approaches and strategies. Similarly, adopting an emphasis on being cultur- ally sustaining may make students feel more comfortable and accepted, leading to increased motivation, and, perhaps, greater accomplishment. Nevertheless, there is evidence that pedagogy that adapts to the cultural patterns of the home and community does not necessarily help ELs and/or SLIFE achieve academic success (see, e.g., Nieto, 2018.) These shifts alone do not in and of themselves produce school success in which students reach their potential academically.

This next section explores how culturally responsive and sustaining teaching is operationalized in the service of effective instruction for SLIFE, namely through the Mutually Adaptive Learning Paradigm (MALP). In MALP, a new learning paradigm is created by taking elements from the two paradigms examined in Chapter 2. This means that in MALP we incorporate what is most essential for SLIFE into our classrooms: being culturally responsive and sustaining—while at the same time retaining what is most essential from the learning paradigm of formal education in our classrooms as well, preparing SLIFE for success in their new instructional setting. The result is a mindset in which both SLIFE and teachers accommodate and honor the key priorities of the other. In this way, SLIFE have a sense of security from the familiar aspects of their own learning paradigm as they are introduced to the new priorities of the formal learning paradigm, thereby reducing their sense of cultural dissonance.

The MALP instructional approach rests on the three components that can be seen as the basis of any learning paradigm, as discussed in Chapter 2.

In MALP, for Component A, Conditions for Learning, we adapt as *we accept the conditions* and priorities for learning from the SLIFE paradigm, immediate relevance and interconnectedness. For Component B, Processes for Learning, both teachers and students adapt to *combine the processes* from the two paradigms: shared responsibility with individual responsibility, and oral transmission with the written word. For Component C, Activities for Learning, SLIFE must adapt as they *target new activities* requiring the performance of decontextualized tasks based on academic ways of thinking (see Figure 3.2).

We would like to emphasize that MALP is not a remedial version of the formal education learning paradigm. At the same time, this does not mean that instruction is aligned exclusively with the learning paradigm of SLIFE, because, as we have noted, this would prevent them from succeeding in formal education. Instead, MALP is a carefully crafted approach to instruction that takes elements from each of the two paradigms and creates instruction that is inclusive of SLIFE, while at the same time making formal education accessible to them. How exactly is this accomplished?

To understand, we turn first to a familiar distinction in education: the affective and cognitive domains. The conditions for learning are clearly part of a student's affect while learning. If the conditions are not in place, the teacher will find it difficult to reach the student, possibly leading to disengagement. Therefore, we will need to accept SLIFE conditions for learning as part of our new approach. This is our incorporation of the original soil that we referred to earlier.

Likewise, the processes for learning also fall into the affective domain. If we fail to include the preferred processes of SLIFE for learning, then the very strengths they need to make learning happen will no longer be available. If these students do not see the classroom as a place where oral transmission and shared responsibility are actively supported, they are less likely to feel motivated. As a result, they are more likely to feel marginalized, both in terms of their willingness to participate, and in terms of their feeling empowered to take on the work of the classroom. In short, they will feel alone, isolated, and ultimately, discouraged. Thus, we will need to incorporate these processes for learning, oral transmission and shared responsibility, in our new approach. Again, we are being cognizant of the original soil that we bring into our classroom so that students can thrive and grow there.

In reviewing SLIFE processes for learning, oral transmission and shared responsibility, we note that formal education requires *individual accountability*. There are many situations, notably assessments, where formal education demands that each student demonstrate individual mastery apart from other students. If SLIFE rely solely on shared responsibility, they will face difficulties when they are expected to demonstrate their mastery. The solution is to combine the two processes from both paradigms, shared responsibility with individual accountability. By continually drawing on both of these processes, we can work with SLIFE to gradually become more comfortable being responsible as individual learners for completing activities and assessments.

Similarly, with oral transmission and the written word, we need to transition SLIFE to print-based literacy as the primary means for accessing, building, and sharing new information and knowledge, as well as for demonstrating mastery, as on assessments. Again, we combine these processes to effect a transition in which SLIFE are comfortable in both worlds—the world of orality and the world of the written word. For example, SLIFE can work in small groups or pairs on an assignment, with steps that also require them to produce something individually. Such assignments could involve students working in pairs to practice reading a text out loud and answering questions about what they have read. Each student would be responsible for noting where their partner had trouble recognizing and/or pronouncing a word or phrase. They would also read out loud and answer the questions orally together, but write out their responses individually. Here we see the combining of both processes, the oral with the written, and group responsibility with individual accountability.

Having explored the conditions and processes from the SLIFE learning paradigm and the processes for learning from the formal education paradigm, we see how the MALP approach is mutually adaptive. We turn now to the hidden challenge of formal education—one that, as both members of a culture permeated by the paradigm of formal education, as well as purveyors of this paradigm, we find exceedingly difficult to recognize, just like the assumptions we explored at length in Chapter 1.

The hidden challenge we address here is the formal schema of decontextualized tasks and associated ways of thinking. In Chapter 2 we introduced the concept of schema by first reciting the months of the year as we always do, that is, in the order they come in the year, and then trying to do so alphabetically. Reciting them by order in the year posed no problem because it entailed a familiar formal schema. Reciting them alphabetically, on the other hand, was much more difficult because it involved an unfamiliar schema.

Returning now to the hidden challenge, we take for granted that the tasks and ways of thinking we have our students engage in to develop, build, and demonstrate mastery will be familiar, except in the earliest years of primary school. Common decontextualized tasks include sorting, matching, filling in tables, constructing graphs, multiple choice or true/false questions, and completing graphic organizers, to name only a few. Underlying each decontextualized task is one or more academic ways of thinking. For example, the academic way of thinking underlying a Venn diagram is comparing and contrasting; underlying filling in a table might be analysis, classification, or justification. Readers may be familiar with Bloom's Taxonomy, higher order thinking skills (HOTS), or other similar concepts that have a hierarchical view of thinking processes (see DeCapua, 2021; 2022; DeCapua, Marshall & Tang, 2020 for more examples and discussion). What these conceptualizations all share is that ways of thinking are rooted in the paradigm of formal education and, at least at the lower levels of the hierarchies, are assumed to be universal and are taken for granted (Ventura et al., 2008). However, SLIFE have a different learning paradigm and ways of thinking than those required in formal education. For example, defining is considered part of the act of remembering, and yet, for SLIFE, defining a tree is neither a common learning task nor a meaningful one (see Chapter 5). Summarizing is considered part of one's ability to demonstrate understanding, but is another new task for SLIFE. Their formal schemata may be such that when they categorize objects, for instance, they will do so based on their prior learning and life experiences rather than on abstract categories determined by what formal education, grounded in science-based logic and reasoning, has identified as shared characteristics.

Consider for instance, *women, fire, and other dangerous things*. Would you consider these three as composing a category? Did it grab your attention? Perhaps it caused you to chuckle. Now how about *sonnets, haiku, and limericks*? Did you have the same reaction? Why or why not? The first example comes from the title of a book (Lakoff, 1987). The author of this book is using an example of categorization found in an Australian aboriginal language. The three items, women, fire, and other dangerous things, comprise a category based on significantly different characteristics than those we expect to see and that to us seem rather jarring when grouped together as a class of things. In the second example, on the other hand, sonnets, haiku, and limericks are three types of poetry, which we categorize differently from dramas, plays, or biographies. But think about why the second example might be considered to be "correct" or "good" while the first one might not? It relates to what cognitive pathways – ways of thinking – are important in one's world, and recognizing that these are not universal. And for SLIFE, abstract categorization methods are part of the hidden challenge of formal education, along with the decontextualized tasks themselves.

Once we realize that academic ways of thinking are learned and practiced through decontextualized tasks starting in the earliest years of formal primary education, and that these are not familiar to SLIFE regardless of their age, we understand the necessity of explicitly teaching both the tasks and the academic ways of thinking.

Just as we do for the conditions and processes for learning, we will find ways to use the original soil in our teaching of these activities. In the MALP approach this entails using familiar language and content while delivering instruction that targets academic ways of thinking and decontextualized tasks. Building on familiar content and familiar language ensures that, in classroom activities, we balance the familiar and unfamiliar. That is, when the activity itself is the focus, we do not add the additional challenge of learning new content and/ or new language. Here again we see the valuable role of translanguaging and transculturing when working to master and ultimately internalize academic ways of thinking and new decontextualized tasks.

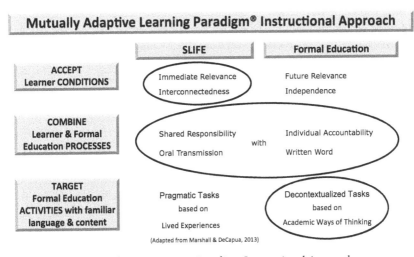

Figure 3.2. Mutually Adaptive Learning Paradigm Instructional Approach

Component A: Teachers Accept Students' Conditions for Learning

In the Mutually Adaptive Learning Paradigm, teachers must first accept the conditions for learning from the learning paradigm of SLIFE: *immediate relevance* and *interconnectedness*. MALP takes as a starting point these conditions as priorities for SLIFE, and we adapt our instruction to accommodate them. As these two priorities are conditions that create a climate where SLIFE feel able and ready to learn, we consider how to design instruction and create classroom communities in such a way as to honor these conditions. By accepting the condition of immediate relevance to their students' lives, teachers initially focus on incorporating familiar material into their lessons, making associations between past experiences and current life situations of SLIFE and the new teaching material. Through interconnectedness, students learn about their teachers and about each other, their families, cultures, and prior experiences, sharing their funds of knowledge. Accepting the condition of interconnectedness also includes instruction that is consistent with Principle 1 of the ICF: Establishing and Maintaining Ongoing Two-Way Communication. When the curriculum is made meaningful by acknowledging and incorporating these two conditions, SLIFE are more likely to engage (Crandall, 2018).

Ensuring Immediate Relevance

In Chapter 2, we introduced the idea that what is considered relevant in formal education is different from the understanding many SLIFE have of relevance. In MALP, relevance means making connections between the pragmatic worldview of SLIFE and the academic world of school; it means making learning relevant to the here and now of students' lives, rather than to some time in the future or to the curriculum. To incorporate immediate relevance, the teacher begins each unit of instruction with how at least some aspects of the material being introduced can be applied to the lives of the students.

Mary Jo, a U.S. high school social studies teacher, writes:

> At this point in the year the class is studying the movement of people westward across what eventually becomes the United States, and the Mexican-American War and Native American conflicts involved in this process. I decided to take the usual lessons and adjust them according to some of the principles I read about in the MALP articles. Following the ideas of MALP, I knew that my lesson needed to be personal and immediately relevant. The easiest way to do this was to begin the lesson with a brief class discussion about why we move to new places, what motivates us to move, how we survive once we arrive. The students shared some very good stories, learning more about each other (building those social relationships) and also sharing some funny experiences they had when they arrived and had to communicate, shop for groceries, etc.

Mary Jo's lesson is not planned simply for motivation but also to give the students specific information and skills they can use. Learning parallels the changes in their lives. This same concept can be taught in other contexts where there is a saga of movement within a geographic area that the students have heard about before and can relate to their own lived experiences.

Nearly all of the curriculum can be viewed through this lens, but it must be a priority in lesson planning, and implemented with intention rather than as an afterthought (see also Ledger & Montero, 2022). Once the stage is set in this way, SLIFE begin to regard education as something related to their lives.

Ensuring Interconnectedness

Interconnectedness, as we saw in Chapter 1, is a central feature of collectivistic cultures from which the majority of SLIFE come. Because group membership and group relationships are primary in such cultures, learning from and with each other, as well as from the teacher, is important. Thus, interconnectedness is also an element of MALP.

To create an interconnected classroom community, teachers infuse instruction with interpersonal elements to build relationships. Although most teachers in formal education, especially those teaching younger students, would feel that this is something any good teacher does, their understanding of "relationship" is not necessarily the same as that of SLIFE. In contemporary societies such as in Australia, Canada, the U.K., and the U.S., people tend to compartmentalize their lives and relationships into work, school, family, and so on. For the most part, teachers consider very personal questions from students to be inappropriate and do not expect or want students to visit them unannounced or call them randomly.

Nevertheless, teachers who have strong relationships with their students in the sense of knowing who they are, their cultures, needs, wants, and aspirations, and who deliver appropriate instruction, are the most effective (Kibler, 2019). They are teachers who take responsibility for both the affective and cognitive domains in the classroom. Being a good teacher is both about best techniques and materials, and about establishing genuine relationships with one's students. Good techniques and materials are important, but these are *tools* of teacher-student relationships and *not ends in themselves* (italics added, Clarke, 2007, p. 131). For most SLIFE, these relationships are a key condition for learning. When SLIFE find themselves in classrooms that do not foster strong interconnectedness, they tend to feel alienated and isolated, increasing their cultural dissonance. Given the importance of personal connection, it is not surprising that research on student disengagement and dropout rates globally, not just on SLIFE, repeatedly underscores the importance of interconnectedness (e.g., Andrews, 2016; Markarova & Herzog, 2013). Support for the first component of MALP, accepting students' conditions for learning, is evident in the research. Sarroub, Pernicek & Sweeney (2007), in their case study of a struggling SLIFE, describe how one teacher especially made social connections with the student, often inquiring about personal topics such as his family or car problems. It is essential that teachers make it a priority to have students relate to them. As we saw earlier in the chapter, Karin, by building interconnectedness with her students who frequently missed school, was able to discover a way for them to communicate with her to determine whether or not they would be able to attend that day (Pastoor, 2015). As you continue reading this book, you will explore how activities and projects within the MALP framework provide opportunities for creating interconnectedness.

Fostering a strong sense of interconnectedness may seem difficult because it requires time to develop student-to-student and teacher-to-student relationships, especially in secondary school settings where subject matter takes center stage and the structure of the school day often precludes extended contact time. Nevertheless, it is essential to make relationships a priority because, in the end, the students become invested in the learning when it is situated in an interconnected learning community created by the teacher, as this next activity illustrates.

Discovery Activity: Teacher-Student Relationship

Phong, a 17-year-old SLIFE from Vietnam, was not a particularly committed student. One day, he came to see Mrs. Higgins in her classroom after school. He spent about an hour asking Mrs. Higgins questions about her work life, her home life, and her general outlook on life as a whole and then left. Mrs. Higgins felt bewildered. She had expected that eventually Phong would come to the point of why he had requested the meeting, perhaps for extra help or to discuss some problem he was having related to school.

The next day in class, Phong was a different student. He was engaged in the lesson, smiled, and was interested in learning the new material. After class, Mrs. Higgins asked him about the change in his behavior and he explained, "Now I know you, I can learn from you."

1. Explain what led to the change in Phong's outlook.
2. How does this relate to the concept of interconnectedness?
3. How does this concept differ from behaviors in formal education, especially in upper grades?

When the two conditions for learning are in place in the classroom, SLIFE are better able to cope with the challenges of learning English, building content knowledge, and literacy skills, and developing academic ways of thinking. This requires that we infuse our lessons with opportunities for fostering interconnectedness and making learning relevant in new ways.

When we incorporate and foster the two major conditions SLIFE want and need, we do not need to sacrifice the goals and objectives of English language development or subject area content mastery. By addressing these affective factors—the conditions for learning—SLIFE can turn more constructively to the academic factors. Because they can find what they seek in terms of interconnectedness in the classroom and the immediate relevance to their lives of the material they are learning, they are more likely to take the extra steps to learn new material and try new learning strategies (DeCapua & Marshall, 2020; Marshall & DeCapua, 2018).

Component B: Students and Teachers Combine Processes for Learning from Both Paradigms

The second component of MALP is to combine the processes for learning. By combining, we incorporate the processes that SLIFE normally use—*shared responsibility* and *oral transmission*—into our lessons with the processes SLIFE must master to achieve in formal education, namely *individual accountability* and the *written word*. We combine the processes for learning to assist SLIFE in their transition from the familiar to the unfamiliar. By careful infusion of the MALP approach into instruction, we create bridges between shared responsibility and individual accountability, and between oral transmission and the written word. In using MALP, we intentionally and conscientiously accept the importance of sharing with peers and the oral mode of passing along new information. We realize how new, and even threatening, individual accountability may be for SLIFE, and how alien and disorienting the heavy emphasis on the written word in any form may be.

At this juncture, you may be feeling somewhat confused and wondering exactly what the difference might be between interconnectedness, which we considered earlier as a condition for learning, and shared responsibility, which we are discussing here as a process for learning. Let's think about this for a moment. Remember how you read about Phong and his need to have a sense of a relationship with his teacher, Mrs. Higgins, before he felt ready to learn from her? Also, remember the emphasis in the Intercultural Communication Framework on a two-way relationship between students and the community? This means that the students hear from the school, but also that the school community hears from—and listens to—the students. These examples highlight the concept of interconnectedness, where people feel they are linked or part of a *web* of relationships. Shared responsibility, on the other hand, refers to the idea of people working jointly to accomplish something, such as a task. It's helping each other to find a solution, get the correct answer, or create a project together (de Souza, 2013). Interconnectedness creates a key foundation for more successful collaboration when students are sharing responsibility. Distinguishing between the two concepts in this way helps deepen our understanding of MALP.

Moving from Shared Responsibility to Individual Accountability

In implementing MALP, teachers consistently combine the familiar process of shared responsibility with the new one of individual accountability. A MALP classroom incorporates much more cooperative work than a traditional secondary classroom. While the cooperative classroom is encouraged and indeed viewed as central to good teaching, especially in the elementary grades (Slavin, 2015; 2018), far too often teachers continue to teach traditionally. This is even more true as students move up through the grades (Trumbull et al., 2020). Allowing and encouraging SLIFE to share and learn informally from each other and from the teacher fosters a sense of the classroom as a community. With cooperative learning, teachers need to ensure that students are able to effectively participate, as well as remain on task. When the task or materials are too difficult and not adequately scaffolded, students' attention will wander and/ or they may become discouraged and disengaged. When we introduce a task requiring individual accountability, it is crucial that we explicitly identify what students are to complete on their own. We model this first, step by step, so that the SLIFE see exactly what is expected of them. Initially, tasks requiring individual accountability should be short, to give the students an opportunity to become accustomed to working alone. This procedure differs greatly from the more common practice of using group work for low stakes tasks and individual work for high stakes tasks, which negatively impacts SLIFE because they don't necessarily understand why in the latter situation they can no longer rely on other classmates for help.

Moving from Oral Transmission to the Written Word

SLIFE, who have different needs from ELs with age-appropriate reading and writing skills and educational backgrounds, require different methods and approaches to literacy. Because of the perception of their emergent reading and writing skills as a deficiency, they may suffer psychological barriers in developing these skills, such as frustration, anxiety, and low self-esteem (Gagné et al., 2018; Gahungu, Gahungu & Luseno, 2011).When, however, SLIFE receive appropriate instruction, practice, and support, reading and writing become powerful tools that can change their lives in a meaningful way, and are not merely requirements of an unfamiliar and alien school system (Marshall, DeCapua & Antolini, 2010; Montero, Newmaster & Ledger, 2014). Much as the Brazilian educational philosopher Paulo Freire (2014) has argued in his research on adult literacy learners, when print-based literacy functions as an empowering action, developing reading and writing skills becomes meaningful and increasingly desirable.

An essential process within MALP is to transition SLIFE to the primacy of print-based literacy in the learning paradigm of formal education by combining oral transmission and the written word. In so doing, teachers scaffold the transition to print by building on the strength of SLIFE, oral communication. Here we emphasize again, as we did in Chapter 2, that including activities that use oral transmission is not simply a matter of making oral language integral to completing activities in the classroom. Oral transmission goes beyond reciting, repeating, or talking; it refers to the act of conveying information and knowledge and entails a great deal of built-in redundancy to help hearers learn and retain the information being conveyed. Teachers can incorporate oral transmission by infusing lessons with such devices as call and response questions: "What's the first step you need to do?" or "Now what are you going to have to do for this assignment?" These prompts could also serve to build in familiarity with classroom routines: "What do you do when you need help in class?" or "Where do you go to find __?" We need to provide such devices to deliver oral instruction effectively given that SLIFE are accustomed to oral language that embeds devices for retention. One caveat with respect to oral transmission is that, similar to the combining of collaborative and individual work, we must be sure to provide many low stakes opportunities for students to engage solely with print and not wait until high-stakes testing situations, for example, to remove the support of the oral mode.

Component C: Students Learn New Classroom Activities

For Component C, the final, and perhaps most critical component of MALP, students must learn how to engage in new *decontextualized tasks* and associated *academic ways of thinking*. As we saw earlier, these tasks and activities are integral to the learning paradigm of formal education, as well as part of daily life in contemporary society. However, we cannot assume that SLIFE will be familiar with either, and we must therefore explicitly teach both. Because these are often assumed and expected rather than made explicit in the classroom, we refer to them here as the hidden challenge of classroom learning for SLIFE. We can think of addressing this hidden challenge as the primary rationale for

MALP, and we can consider the other elements of MALP as forming a cluster of supports to ensure this challenge can be effectively met.

In the MALP approach, teachers introduce and practice decontextualized tasks and their underlying academic ways of thinking, scaffolding them using familiar language and content. By controlling for language and content, SLIFE can focus on new activities for learning, namely the decontextualized tasks and their associated academic ways of thinking.

We now consider how the MALP approach includes a pathway for students to experience these new ways of thinking. To do this, we turn once again to schema theory.

The instructor's task is essentially to build new schemata. Just as developing literacy skills requires a set of new schemata, so too does developing an academic mindset and the academic ways of thinking concomitant with that mindset. A key to improving students' abilities to engage in decontextualized tasks and associated academic ways of thinking is for them to do these new activities repeatedly with different information and within different contexts. It is through extended practice, as in the MALP approach, that SLIFE become proficient at academic ways of thinking, which are closely tied to background knowledge (Slavin, 2018). Thus, it is critical that teachers of SLIFE help these students both acquire content knowledge and develop their academic ways of thinking while at the same time developing academic language proficiency. The question is: How do teachers do this?

Let's take the example of a basic decontextualized task commonly used in classrooms for students, namely, matching terms and definitions. In this type of task, the items are intentionally placed in a non-matched order on two sides of the page. Although we see this as a "normal" task, for SLIFE it represents a challenge. The presentation alone is confusing for them as it is set up to be viewed both vertically on each side as well horizontally across the page. In teaching students what a matching task is and how to go about doing it, the instructor needs to isolate the concept of matching from any other confusing elements of the activity, such as the language being used and the content being drawn upon in creating the items.

Danielle, a MALP-trained teacher, did this by adding a matching activity at the end of a project on Hispanic heritage (See Chapter 8), in which her students had all shared products or practices from their specific backgrounds or those they were familiar with. She had them each create a matched pair, consisting of one item they had shared with their peers and the name of their culture group. Then the class produced two columns, one for the items and one for the culture groups. Danielle then cut them up and mixed each of the two sets of items together, and took a photo of these mixed-up columns. At this point, Danielle had the students find the matching pairs, which they did first as a manipulative activity by physically moving the items into one column or the other. Then, as a second step, she had them draw lines across the two columns. As a last step, Danielle gave the class the same task in a traditional format using the same material. She numbered the cultural practices in the first column and used letters to label the list of culture groups in the other column. This showed SLIFE how such an activity normally appears in classroom materials. In each step, once the pairs were matched, Danielle took another photo showing them all lined up. The result was a series of matched columns, one simply in order, the next out of order with lines drawn across the columns, and the last, also out of order but with numbers and letters. (For a complete presentation of Danielle's MALP project, see Chapter 8.)

This type of explicit teaching gives SLIFE a sense of confidence in completing matching as a decontextualized task based on an academic way of thinking. Similarly, each new task is introduced with familiar language and content so that students can focus on the task itself. Schema theory is instructive here. The new schema being built in this case is a formal schema—having to do with the way information is organized, presented, processed, and retrieved. When a formal schema is the focus, as in Component C of MALP, it is best to design the activity without any other new schemata. That is the reason to use familiar language and content as Danielle did in the case of teaching matching. This balancing of the schemata needs to happen in order for SLIFE to become well-versed and confident in "doing school." It may be helpful to remember that once each individual new schema has been introduced, practiced, and mastered with familiar language and content, it can be used going forward in all subject areas and with more difficult language.

A deep understanding of the hidden challenge underlying Component C of MALP depends upon appreciating how the three types of schemata interrelate. Commonly, classroom activities consist of all three schemata: the *content* is presented in a particular *language* and *organized* in a specific way. For example, in her social studies class, Kristy is teaching a unit on volcanoes. The students have been reading about four different volcanoes. They can name each volcano and describe it. But Kristy is also expecting them to learn the name of the four types of volcanoes each one represents, the characteristics of each type, and how they are alike or different. Without decontextualized tasks or academic ways of thinking, students would learn all about each one separately as individual volcanoes. However, using a school-based mindset, this is not sufficient for mastery of the material. The individual volcanoes must be classified as to type, their traits identified and categorized, and their similarities and differences noted—all formal schemata. For students who have already been initiated into academic ways of thinking, the new material will be the content and some of the language as well, but for many SLIFE the activities themselves will also be new.

To illustrate the presence of the three schemata in all classroom activities, consider the following examples:

Discovery Activity: Academic Ways of Thinking Using Familiar Language and Content

> Classroom Activity 1: Write a science lab report in academic English.
> Classroom Activity 2: Tell a culturally traditional folktale in your preferred language.

1. Identify the three schemata in each activity. What is the content? The language? The formal schema?
2. Which activity would be easier for SLIFE? Explain why you made this decision.

In Classroom Activity 1, SLIFE will find all three schemata unfamiliar. First, the *language* is not only English, but academic English. Second, the *content* is new and relatively unfamiliar because it is based on a science experiment from this week's lesson. Finally, the *formal* schema is unfamiliar because the SLIFE must write a lab report, which has a very specific rhetorical organization and form.

In Classroom Activity 2, all three schemata are familiar to SLIFE: the *language* is familiar because it is the student's preferred language; the *content* is familiar because it asks SLIFE to recount a folktale they know; and the *formal schema* is familiar as well because it is a story from their own culture and based on a rhetorical form familiar to them. This type of activity could be an opportunity for students to share with others and might be used in a bilingual program for home language arts development. Note, however, that such an activity by itself is not enough in MALP because it does not practice and develop the academic ways of thinking required for Component C.

The balancing of schemata requires that the new formal schema of the academic task be the primary unfamiliar aspect of the activity. Therefore, to help SLIFE learn the academic ways of thinking of Component C, teachers introduce only the new formal schemata, while controlling that the language and content are familiar, a practice valuable for native speakers and essential for SLIFE. A coin collector, for example, is more likely to be able to work out a problem on fractions if the problem is framed in terms of exchanging money than if the problem is framed in terms of calculating the efficiency of an engine, because in the former the language and content are familiar (Willingham, 2009, p. 91).

Building on this example, each task that teachers assign for SLIFE should occur in the context of familiar language and content schemata, allowing SLIFE to focus on the decontextualized task and associated academic ways of thinking without the added complications of new language and content. While SLIFE certainly need to develop their language proficiency and subject matter knowledge, from the MALP perspective, language and content learning are separate from developing and practicing decontextualized tasks and academic ways of thinking. We emphasize again that we must explicitly teach these decontextualized tasks, an approach that goes beyond simply teaching the mechanics of true/false and multiple choice questions, matching, filling in graphic organizers, and so on. We must also make clear to students what is intended in these tasks, their purpose, and the thinking underlying them. Otherwise, SLIFE are likely to see these tasks as without a rationale and feel confused or even tricked by them. Using the MALP approach can help them to see how these tasks are used in formal education to develop their academic ways of thinking and ensure their mastery of concepts and subject matter.

To summarize, the MALP instructional approach incorporates elements from both the learning paradigm of SLIFE and the learning paradigm of formal education, thereby creating a third learning paradigm in which both sides adapt. In this way, neither the students nor the teachers must completely alter their approach to the classroom. By accepting the conditions for learning from the SLIFE learning paradigm, teachers adapt their instruction to accommodate the needs of their students. By teachers explicitly combining processes from both paradigms, SLIFE more easily make the transition to the processes of the learning paradigm of formal education–individual accountability and print. By scaffolding activities that introduce and practice academic ways of thinking, SLIFE learn to think academically, not only pragmatically.

MALP has, then, explicitly addressed the three ICF principles for addressing cultural dissonance—maintaining two-way communication, identifying priorities, and building associations. The communication element is evident in Component A, for which the teacher establishes interconnectedness in the MALP classroom. The identification of priorities from both cultures is evident in the way in which MALP accommodates some priorities from the SLIFE learning paradigm, while requiring SLIFE to adapt to key priorities from the learning paradigm of formal education—individual accountability, the written word, and academic tasks. In Component B teachers encourage the development of individual accountability and familiarity with print by associating them with the familiar processes for SLIFE—shared responsibility and oral transmission. In Component C, teachers introduce academic ways of thinking through academic learning activities based on familiar language and content to assist SLIFE in making associations, even as they develop new schemata. Finally, building associations between the familiar and unfamiliar is clearly integral to both Components B and C. By creating a MALP classroom, teachers can maximize the opportunity for SLIFE to succeed in their new educational setting. The MALP approach ensures that both teachers and students work together to create a classroom environment that is a positive, challenging, yet supportive setting for this population.

We have seen that focusing on academic instruction by itself is not sufficient for SLIFE to become academically successful. When teachers value their students' cultures and languages, they demonstrate an openness and willingness to accept differences. The social nature of the classroom must be taken into account as well. Teachers who truly know their students, their experiences, and their cultural backgrounds will be able to utilize this knowledge to better facilitate learning. Teachers who have achieved notable success in challenging teaching situations do not adhere to one teaching philosophy and style of lesson delivery, and they often use several. However, what they all share is that they care about each and every student, have strong relationships with their students, and are sensitive to issues in their students' lives outside the classroom (DeNicolo et al., 2017; Levi, 2019). In being culturally responsive, instructors using MALP take the first step by listening and learning from their students and then responding to them by incorporating their priorities into the paradigm. To extend the notion of creating fertile spaces discussed earlier, in being not only culturally responsive but also culturally sustaining, this new learning paradigm seeks to change the learning context—the soil environment that sustains the flower, and not the flower itself—thereby revealing the rationale for MALP. A mutually adaptive instructional approach does this by incorporating a sociocultural perspective. From such a perspective, language, learning, and meaning are interconnected. Subsequent chapters explore more specifically how MALP is implemented in SLIFE classes.

For Further Exploration

1. Getting to know each other and feeling a sense of interconnectedness is important for all students. Explain how this is even more important for SLIFE and why it might be more difficult or unusual at the secondary level than in earlier grades. Design some ways that you could increase your interconnectedness with your SLIFE. What might you do differently that would help them to feel connected to you and more able to learn from you?

2. Ms. Biscoglio, when presented with the notion of interconnectedness and MALP, feels it doesn't apply to her:

I'm already very close with my students. I believe that relationships are the key to learning and I already know that. This isn't a helpful concept for me as I already incorporate this condition into my classroom every day.

    a. Explain how interconnectedness as SLIFE perceive it is different from relationships that all good teachers have with their students.

    b. Discuss how you might make the concept of interconnectedness clearer and more comprehensible to Ms. Biscoglio and others like her.

    c. Explain how interconnectedness is different from shared responsibility.

3. Design an activity for students that requires them to create an oral version of something presented in print. Do the reverse as well. What do you notice is different in the two activities you have designed?

4. Ms. Lopez has the students work in pairs on a regular basis for part of each math lesson. However, even though each student has a partner, she allows them to consult with other students as well. She has trained them to guide each other and not give the answer—a skill they are proud of mastering. Because she has focused on teaching the steps of problem solving, they help each other with a given step and then let the other student work on that step. Translanguaging is used for this purpose, but the students must use English when the class comes back together. Because some SLIFE are better at math and some are better at English, there is a great deal of sharing in Ms. Lopez's classroom. How does Ms. Lopez's approach reflect the MALP classroom? Explain your answer by referring to the components of MALP.

5. Martha McGloin has a class of SLIFE who have had attendance issues. This by itself is a statement about priorities, as we discussed earlier in the chapter when looking at Karin and her Afghan students. Here is how Martha addressed the same issue but turned it into a MALP project:

Martha has noticed that when she asks the students the reason for their absence, they often give one that is not considered acceptable in most schools. She has set up a chart in her classroom where students can add their reason for being absent. Together the students discuss the reason, taking into account whether it is acceptable given the mandates of school attendance, as well as the priorities of the students. Then Martha helps the students enter the reason onto a card that is red, yellow, or green, indicating the acceptability rating decided on after class discussion. Examples of each color are as follows:

Red

- I wanted to see my Dad's friend.
- I was asleep so late I couldn't come.
- It was raining.

Yellow

- I had to interpret for my aunt.
- I had to go with my parents because nobody could pick me up at 3:30.
- I had to help my brother when he went to the eye doctor.

Green

- I had a fever.
- I had a toothache and went to the dentist.
- I threw up.

Reflect on Martha's Attendance Project:

a. Why do you think students might have originally thought that reasons categorized as "red" were acceptable ones for not coming to school?

b. Why might the reasons that students categorized as "yellow" be considered acceptable or unacceptable? Think about our previous discussions of collectivism, as well as priorities.

c. What elements of MALP can you identify in Martha's class project on attendance?

d. What about the ICF? Do you see that Martha is also using this framework to inform her work with her class of SLIFE? Be specific about how ICF principles are in evidence here.

4. Infusing Lessons with MALP

This chapter introduces readers to the ways in which MALP can be infused into lessons. We will see how two teachers, Christina and Rick, using content-based language instruction, incorporated MALP to make their lessons more effective for SLIFE. We will examine in detail Christina's three-lesson sequence and how she included each element of MALP. We will also examine Rick's hands-on math lessons and how he used a checklist designed specifically for this approach.

An extremely important challenge for SLIFE is the need to attain grade-level performance at the same time they are struggling to master English, develop literacy skills, and adjust to school culture. To accomplish this, they must focus from the very beginning on developing academic English in addition to everyday conversational skills because academic English is the language of schooling. A way to facilitate academic language proficiency is to introduce such language through content-based instruction (CBI), alternatively referred to as either Content and Language Integrated Learning (CLIL) (Cenoz, 2015; Snow & Brinton, 2019), or the Sheltered Instruction Observation Protocol (SIOP®) (Echevarria, Vogt & Short, 2016). In these approaches, instructors teach language through content from different subject areas, often through thematic units or project-based learning (see Chapter 5). These approaches, when implemented in conjunction with MALP, are especially valuable for high school SLIFE since they have so few years to achieve content-knowledge parity with their peers. While developing academic language through content is properly the focus of instruction, SLIFE also need to develop competence in the academic ways of thinking and decontextualized tasks that most of their peers have been engaging in since the early grades.

Earlier chapters revealed that the formal schemata of school create the major barrier to success for SLIFE and that academic ways of thinking and decontextualized tasks exemplify these schemata most clearly. Although SLIFE are acquiring new language and content, if the formal schemata used to teach the new language and content are unfamiliar, they will be unable to access the instruction in the way that other ELs can. The third component of MALP, Component C, Activities for Learning, calls for teachers to introduce and practice academic ways of thinking. These ways of thinking may be completely new, or may be a more complex version of one already introduced and practiced. Component C also requires that teachers develop students' skills in completing the decontextualized tasks used in school to develop and demonstrate mastery of these ways of thinking.

The next section shows how Christina, who teaches ESL and social studies for SLIFE, infuses MALP into her lessons, with a particular focus on Component C, yet not neglecting the other components.

Social Studies Scenario

This week, Christina is teaching her self-contained SLIFE class about the U.S. presidential election. She has already worked with her students on the concept of individual voting as part of the democratic system and how that differs from having a group reach a consensus, as some of the students are used to from their experience in their home countries. She is trying to convey the idea that it is the *population* of a U.S. state, not its physical size, that determines how many votes it is given to choose the president. The underlying concept is that of the electoral college, a difficult concept even for many students in the U.S. To avoid getting into details while still helping them understand that there is an additional step that affects the outcome of the presidential election, Christina introduces only the vocabulary items *state, population,* and *electoral votes.* Her twin goals are to follow the mandated social studies curriculum without overwhelming her students with too much information and to develop her students' academic ways of thinking, such as compare and contrast.

To have enough time for the students to engage in a culminating activity for this sequence of lessons, Christina uses double periods of ESL and social studies. For such an activity, a minimum of three to five periods is usually required.

Christina begins with her language and content objectives for this six-period, three-day lesson sequence. In addition to her objectives for English language proficiency development and her objectives for social studies, Christina will introduce or further develop academic ways of thinking through an unfamiliar task. Over the course of three days, she focuses on this task to ensure that the SLIFE become accustomed to this new way of thinking. Here is an overview of her three-day plan.

Christina's Three-Day Plan for her Self-Contained SLIFE Class
Day 1: Building background about the election and the candidates
Day 2: Learning to use the internet to find information on current events; collecting and recording data for two states
Day 3: Comparing and contrasting electoral votes for two states; creating and sharing a poster with the information

Christina prepares for the lesson sequence by finding websites about the election that she has preselected for clarity, visuals, and minimal text. She also finds one or two websites in the home languages of her students whenever possible. She bookmarks these sites for them so that they will be able to search among the sites from a webpage she has created for the class. Christina also prepares a sample poster to be used as a model for the ones that her students will complete as their culminating activity for these lessons.

Day 1

Christina asks her students to name any U.S. state they have heard of or have some connection to in their personal lives; the class then goes together to that state's official website—to see pictures, to see the state on the map, and to learn something new about that state. The students and Christina discuss how the size of a state does not necessarily correlate with the number of people who live there. New Jersey, for instance, is much smaller than Montana, yet New Jersey has a much higher population. Once they have viewed several states on the internet, Christina shows them a chart with the names of the states they have asked her about and two numbers: population and number of electoral votes.

State	Population	# of Electoral Votes
New York	19,299,981	29
Pennsylvania	12,804,123	20
California	39,613,493	55
Texas	29,730,311	38

Next, Christina asks the class if they know who is running for president in the upcoming election and if they know anything about the candidates. They talk and share ideas while Christina makes notes on chart paper with key words from the students' contributions. The students are not only allowed but encouraged to use translanguaging, calling upon their whole repertoire of languages when they don't know the English words or when they are explaining a concept to a fellow student. They also help each other say the words in English.

After Christina has finished writing their notes, the students read them aloud together. They then practice forming sentences based on the notes. She has put links on her webpage to some relevant websites for them to browse when they go to the lab the next day, and has put the notes the students made together up on the wall. These notes are designed to guide the students in finding out more on their own.

Day 2

Today this self-contained ESL social studies class for SLIFE meets in the computer lab. Christina gives each student a graphic organizer to complete. She asks them to work with a partner and gives each pair two different states to research. They locate their states from Christina's list of sites. Next, they collect the data they will analyze: the population of each state and the number of electoral votes, pictures of the state, the shape of the state, and the state's size in relation to other states as seen on a U.S. map that Christina has hung on a wall. To differentiate instruction for more advanced students, Christina suggests that they collect other information that they find interesting about the two states. After the SLIFE have had time to conduct their research, Christina asks each student to choose one of the two states and to collect any extra information the pair would like to have. Each pair prints out at least two photos and the shape of the state from the website.

Day 3

The students are back in their classroom. Christina shows them her sample poster, in which she has compared and contrasted two states. She tells them that they will produce a similar poster. She points to her completed poster as she explains each item: the title, the names of the states, the pictures, the shapes and sizes, the population figure, and the number of electoral votes these states have. At the bottom of her poster Christina has composed a compare and contrast sentence using *although*:

> *Although* Wyoming is larger than Virginia, Virginia has more electoral votes because it has more people.

After she finishes pointing to the different parts of her poster, she has each student come to her poster, point to an item on the poster, and explain what that item is. Yaneit comes up first, points to the picture of Virginia on the poster, and says, "This Virginia, I know, my aunt live there." Yaneit volunteers to be first because she can relate to one picture personally and wants to share this with the rest of the class.

Christina's compare and contrast sentence at the bottom of the poster is not an easy one for SLIFE. In order to help her students understand this sentence, Christina provides scaffolding, showing the SLIFE how each part of the sentence comes from the data on the poster by pointing to the sentence and the data as she reads. She elicits the data orally and asks one student to write each sentence on the board, based on sentence frames.

Sentence frames are mini-templates into which students insert the appropriate words (Nattinger & DeCarrico, 1992). Such frames allow students to see and produce accurate sentence patterns—that is, grammatically correct sentences—without becoming bogged down in grammar rules. While sentence frames have become an accepted best practice for all ELs, these frames are especially important in scaffolding writing skills for SLIFE. Christina uses frames like the following as scaffolding for this lesson:

(*name of state A*) has_____people and_____electoral votes.

While many ELs may succeed even without such techniques, SLIFE most likely will not, given that they need additional help in accessing academic ways of thinking.

After they have worked through the various statements, the students are ready to understand Christina's compare and contrast statement about her two states: *Although Wyoming is larger than Virginia, Virginia has more electoral votes because it has more people.* Once the students are comfortable with what Christina expects to see on their posters, each pair works on preparing a poster with visuals, data, and a compare and contrast statement. When all the students have completed their posters, the pairs take turns presenting their posters to the rest of the class. Each person in the pair talks about one of the two states. The pair chooses another student in the class to read the final compare and contrast statement they have written at the bottom of their poster.

Discussion of Christina's Lessons

We now look carefully at Christina's three lessons to see how she has infused the three components of MALP: A, Accept the Conditions; B, Combine the Processes; and C, Target New Activities. We also see how she applies the elements of each component. Christina has incorporated one condition for learning, *immediate relevance*, from three different aspects: current events, geography, and cultural background, in addition to the social studies curriculum content.

In this way, each student may find one or another perspective more compelling. As the topic is the election, those students who follow the news or hear about the news from others may become more enthusiastic about the activity. To bring them closer to the topic, Christina selects their own state, New York, as one of the states for modeling the activity.

Another strategy to make lessons more immediately relevant is to capitalize on the natural links across disciplines that are often ignored in secondary school classrooms. Because this lesson sequence involves numbers, Christina found ways to collaborate with the math teacher. In the math class, the students have been learning about rounding numbers so Christina asks the math teacher to use the population figures from the students' posters about the states as examples. In addition to showing SLIFE how what they are learning in one class may assist them with what is going on in another, this type of collaborative effort among teachers gives the students an opportunity to revisit and practice concepts. While making connections across content areas is important for all students, such redundancy and reinforcement is especially important for SLIFE. In addition, it demonstrates that their teachers also have an ongoing two-way relationship, bringing us to the second condition for learning, interconnectedness.

Christina's lesson sequence contains many opportunities for her students to develop and maintain *interconnectedness* with her and with each other. Over the three days of this project, the SLIFE had personal connections to various states that came up in the internet research. They were encouraged to select states with which they had some family connection. Claude wanted to explore Pennsylvania because he had an aunt there; Yolanda wanted to look at Arizona because her brother had been there. During this time, the students wanted to share their opinions about the presidential candidates, especially once they had begun the activity, and they looked for information about them at the sites Christina had bookmarked. In the process of exploring their chosen states and in discussing their opinions about the candidates, the students learned more about each other. As they worked with their partners in their internet search and in creating their posters, the students had further opportunities to connect.

Christina has built in extensive partner work, which SLIFE find familiar and comfortable. The partner work in this activity extends across all three days, and the two students who are working together spend most of their time together, even in the lab where they sit at adjacent computers. Christina encourages them to *share responsibility* and assist each other in finding the information they need. Together they look for the required information about their states, but each of them takes ownership for one state in writing the information on the graphic organizer. This *individual accountability* component is an enhancement to the main task, which is completed together. The poster is a joint effort, although each student will compose parts of it, and they work out together how it will look in terms of layout, content, text, and visuals. Finally, the oral presentation provides an opportunity for them to support each other as they speak to the group and each partner reports on one of the two states. For the poster presentations, another student in the class is called on to read the final statement about the two states. As the statements are similar across posters, the individual student who reads aloud to the class is already familiar with the sentence structure even though the specifics on this poster are new.

Because two students working as partners produce the poster together, the individual student who speaks about a given state has had a great deal of prior scaffolding for this task. The joint effort and social interaction between partners and, when necessary, with other, more knowledgeable classmates, provide essential and indispensable support (Vygotsky, 1978). The partners support each other in collecting, understanding, and preparing the information for the poster so that by the time individual students show the poster to the rest of the class and report the results, they are prepared to do so. In combining the processes for learning through *oral transmission* and the *written word,* Christina consciously delivers her instruction by such techniques as reading aloud and pointing to the words as she reads. She applies these techniques when describing the model poster as she indicates each specific section of the written version. She also reads each of the model sentences from the sentence frames aloud while students follow as she points to the words. For the students, there is constant oral interaction, including translanguaging, as they collect information in the computer lab from the bookmarked sites and as they compose the sentences together that will go on their poster. Finally, for the poster presentations, the students, following their teacher's model from the first day, explain their poster, indicating each section, and ask someone in the class to read the final statement as they point to the words.

After considering which new *academic way of thinking* might be appropriate to link to her social studies lessons on the election, Christina has chosen to work with her class on the concept of comparing and contrasting. Analyzing information in this way is new for them, but she knows they must master it for the many activities, assignments, and assessments they will encounter in school. In finding similarities and differences, she will have to be sure her students focus on specific details about the two states they are researching. For the final statement, which shows that a smaller state may have a larger number of votes, students will need to grasp a *counterintuitive* concept that develops their critical-thinking ability.

Christina also practices using the internet as a tool for accessing data by searching for different information on carefully selected websites. Although her students have used the internet and are familiar with computers, they may not have used websites for learning new subject matter. Scaffolding is needed for them to direct their attention and effort to this decontextualized task. To start, Christina scaffolds the internet searching. Using a webpage with her name on it, the students are directed to preselected sites with links alongside her brief annotations. On these sites, they see familiar language that Christina has prepared for them. Christina's use of bookmarked sites allows the students to go to specific URLs to search for what they need. The sites she has located provide the information they need without a large number of mouse clicks, so they will not become frustrated.

By including three activities: gathering data, comparing and contrasting data, and interpreting data, Christina is building several new formal schemata related to success in school. Critical thinking emerges from this carefully planned sequence of lessons because the result—that a larger state may have fewer votes—is generally counterintuitive to students. This process reinforces the importance of research and data collection to test intuitions and beliefs, an essential component of academic ways of thinking. Recognizing that something may be counterintuitive yet true, will be a key thinking skill they can use across the curriculum and throughout their years in school.

As Christina focuses on these activities, she needs to anchor them in *familiar language and content*. The language needed for collecting and reporting the data on the states is largely familiar to these SLIFE, as are the basic sentence structures they worked with earlier, such as X (*name of state*) has Y (*number of*) people. The only unfamiliar language structure is the statement of contrast with *although*, which is essential for grasping the counterintuitive concept involved in the contrast between densely populated small states and sparsely populated large ones. To make the new structure clear, as we noted earlier, Christina has ensured that each pairing of states results in this contrast. In this way, all the statements are similar and SLIFE can see them recurring, building familiarity with the structure. To scaffold the writing of their own statements, Christina refers the students back to the familiar individual statements of fact that underlie them.

The content for the lesson consists of state names, shapes, sizes, populations, and other data that are concrete and quantifiable, making the information accessible.

Christina asks the students to demonstrate their mastery of this material through a poster which decontextualizes the material and presents it graphically. To prepare them to create this poster, she provides many relevant visuals, including maps and population charts for reference. However, before these visual aids, Christina had taught her students to read maps of their towns, as well as charts on familiar topics. She has also prepared a diagram with the essential information of states and the number of electoral votes they are allotted in choosing the president. Christina and her class work together on understanding and interpreting these visuals, which themselves represent decontextualized tasks.

As a result of Christina's careful preparation using the MALP instructional approach, SLIFE can access the new and difficult academic ways of thinking and decontextualized tasks in her lesson. In this way, SLIFE are not limited in their exposure to such tasks, and they are not expected to perform them without being instructed in how to do so.

We see from this detailed analysis of MALP as it is integrated throughout Christina's lessons that this teacher has successfully internalized the approach and put it to good use in ESL and social studies, producing a six-period, three-day sequence with social studies content and academic English language development for this group of SLIFE.

Using the MALP Teacher Planning Checklist

How can teachers be sure they are using MALP in their lessons the way Christina did? To help, we have developed the MALP Teacher Planning Checklist (see Figure 4.1 and Appendix A). The Checklist is an expedient and systematic way to be sure that the MALP instructional approach is being used. It follows the three components of MALP. For each of these three components, there are elements for the teacher to address while planning lessons and activities for SLIFE. The MALP Checklist consists of a series of statements for teachers to respond to by providing specifics from the lesson for each of the components of MALP. Teachers using the MALP instructional approach look across the entire lesson sequence to see that all the elements of MALP are being implemented, rather than seeing each lesson as a separate freestanding period. Some elements will be more evident in one lesson, others in a different lesson, and still others across different lessons and days.

We turn now to another teacher, Rick, who is teaching MALP-based math lessons and is using the Checklist to be sure all elements of MALP are included. As we follow Rick's lesson, we examine each of the elements of MALP using the Checklist as a guide (see Figure 4.1 or Appendix A).

MALP® Teacher Planning Checklist
Mutually Adaptive Learning Paradigm®

A. Accept Conditions for Learning
A1. I am making this lesson/project immediately relevant to my students' lives. Explain:
A2. I am helping students develop and maintain interconnectedness with each other. Explain:

B. Combine Processes for Learning
B1. I am incorporating both shared responsibility and individual accountability. Explain:
B2. I am scaffolding the written word through oral interaction. Explain:

C. Target New Activities for Learning
C1. I am teaching students to develop academic ways of thinking. Explain:
C2. I am teaching students to engage in decontextualized tasks to demonstrate mastery. Explain:
C3. I am using familiar language and content as scaffolds. Explain:

Revised from © DeCapua, A. & Marshall, H. W. (2011). *Breaking New Ground: Teaching Students with Limited or Interrupted Formal Education in Secondary Schools,* University of Michigan Press, (p.68). For terms and conditions of use, contact information@malpeducation.com

Figure 4.1. MALP Teacher Planning Checklist

Math Scenario

Rick's self-contained math class for SLIFE is struggling with the language of math problems, as do many ELs (Martinello, 2008). In addition, while SLIFE tend to have very rudimentary math skills, they are nonetheless required to participate in a curriculum that demands that they move beyond basic skills. For example, Rick has been working on units of measurement, such as 100 centimeters being equal to one meter. The students have difficulty converting from one unit to another, such as changing 1200 centimeters to 12 meters. Rick plans to use a concrete rather than abstract problem to demonstrate this and to give his students practice in working with units.

One day, Angel, who has been absent for over a week, returns to class, frustrated because he has found a part-time job in home construction but is having problems figuring out what the contractor wants him to do. It turns out that he expects Angel to help him measure floor areas and lay tile and carpet in a new office building.

Using Angel's experience as a starting point, Rick develops a sequence of lessons to help the SLIFE learn the math skills of measurement and converting units of measure. Rick's problem for the class is this: *How many tiles do we need to order for a house?* He begins by bringing in a diagram of his own house with each room labeled. For the purposes of this sequence of lessons, the class will use floor tile for all the rooms in the house. Rick has simplified the floor plan by ignoring closets, kitchen appliances, and other items that would create irregular patterns. In each room on the diagram, Rick writes the dimensions in centimeters and the tile size, large or small, that will be used for that room, as shown in Figure 4.2. Rick needs to introduce a few vocabulary items to the class before they can correctly interpret and read his chart for each room. Rick explains to the class, while holding and pointing to a sample tile, that the symbol "x" stands for the word "by" and that the two dimensions are the "length" and the "width" of each tile.

Rick also provides the class with a chart showing the dimensions of the two sizes of tile.

Tile Size	Tile Dimensions
Large tiles	40 cm. x 40 cm.
Small tiles	20 cm. x 20 cm.

To help SLIFE visualize the problem, Rick brings in samples of tiles of various sizes and photos of rooms with tile floors. In addition, Angel brings in photos of the rooms he is working on for the construction job. Finally, Rick posts a set of instructions with the sequence of steps they need to follow in order to find the number of tiles needed for one room of the house.

STEPS TO SOLVE THE PROBLEM

Follow these steps to solve the problem:

Step 1: Identify the question for the problem.
Step 2: Using the house diagram, identify the dimensions of the room and the tile size needed for the room.
Step 3: Using the tile size and dimensions chart, identify the dimensions of the size needed for the room.
Step 4: Convert the dimensions to all centimeters or all meters.
Step 5: Determine the number of tiles needed for one row in the room.
Step 6: Determine the number of rows of tile needed for the room.
Step 7: Using mathematical operations, determine how many tiles are needed.
Step 8: Write the answer in a sentence and put a box around the number of tiles.

Rick has decided to break the problem into a series of activities designed to culminate in the class providing the number of tiles needed for the entire house. First, Rick and his students work as a class; the SLIFE select one room, the kitchen, to work on together. Rick points out the information given for the kitchen in the house diagram in Figure 4.2, that is, the dimensions of the room and the size of the tile. With Rick's guidance, the SLIFE use the steps listed and refer to the resources he has provided for them to determine the number of tiles needed for the kitchen floor. He provides problems with sentence frames to guide them in this process:

Step 1: We must find out how many tiles we need for the (*name of room*) floor.
Step 2: We see on the diagram of the house that the (*name of room*) is (*dimensions of room*) and (*small / large*) tiles are required.
Step 3: We see from the tile size and dimensions table that the (*small / large*) tiles are (*20 centimeters by 20 centimeters / 40 centimeters by 40 centimeters*).
Step 4: We need to convert the (*name of room*) dimensions to centimeters. The (*name of room*) is (*length*) meters long, equal to (*length*) centimeters. The (*name of room*) is (*width*) meters wide, equal to (*width*) centimeters.
Step 5: Because the (*name of room*) is (*length*) centimeters long, each row has (*number*) tiles.
Step 6: Because the (*name of room*) is (*width*) centimeters wide, we need (*number*) rows of tile.

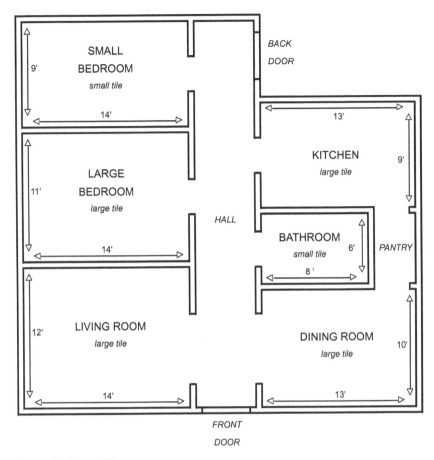

Figure 4.2. House Diagram

Step 7: We need to multiply (*number*) by (*number*) to get (*total number*).
Step 8: We need a total of (*total number*) (*small / large*) tiles for the (*name of room*).

Rick's sample completed sentence frames are:

Step 1: We must find out how many tiles we need for the <u>kitchen</u> floor.
Step 2: We see on the diagram of the house that the <u>kitchen</u> is <u>4.4 meters by 2.8 meters</u> and the <u>large</u> tiles are required.
Step 3: We see from the tile size and dimensions table that the <u>large</u> tiles are <u>40 centimeters by 40 centimeters.</u>
Step 4: We need to convert the <u>kitchen</u> dimensions to centimeters. The <u>kitchen</u> is <u>4.4</u> meters long, equal to <u>440</u> centimeters, and <u>2.8</u> meters wide, equal to <u>280</u> centimeters.

Step 5: The <u>kitchen</u> is <u>440</u> centimeters long, and each <u>large</u> tile is <u>40</u> centimeters long, so each row has <u>11</u> tiles.

Step 6: The <u>kitchen</u> is <u>280</u> centimeters wide, and each <u>large</u> tile is <u>40</u> centimeters wide, so we need <u>7</u> rows of tile.

Step 7: <u>11</u> times <u>7</u> = <u>77</u>.

Step 8: We need a total of <u>77 large</u> tiles for the <u>kitchen</u>.

At this point, we begin our analysis of Rick's lesson using the MALP Teacher Planning Checklist as a guide. The two conditions for learning, immediate relevance and interconnectedness, are the two elements of Component A. The starting point for any teacher using MALP is to reflect on how these conditions will be established and maintained during a given MALP activity.

Discussion of Rick's Lessons

Rick: How am I making this lesson immediately relevant to my students' lives?

In setting up his lessons, Rick has used a variety of techniques for the students to relate to the material. First, he takes his student Angel's experience in construction as his content for the math work. Angel shares information about his job with the class and describes the work he is learning to do for the construction company. Second, Rick shows them a diagram of his own family's house and a photo of a tiled floor in his house. Third, he brings in sample tiles of various sizes. In this way, he links the lesson to real-world experiences.

Rick: How am I helping students develop and maintain interconnectedness and thereby build a learning community?

Like Christina's lessons, Rick's classes also include many chances for students to interact informally and deepen their interconnectedness. During these lessons, Rick found that, in addition to Angel, several other SLIFE had had some experience with building materials. One student had worked as a carpenter's assistant; another was starting an after-school job in a floor-covering stock room. Because Rick allowed for free-flowing conversation, the students increasingly felt that this was a learning community where they, along with Rick, were creating something together. Rick brought in photos of himself in his home workshop, photos showing him with his two siblings in the act of laying tile for a room in his house, and a photo of the room before and after they laid the tile. These photos heightened the sense of interconnectedness between the SLIFE and their teacher. Depending on the teacher's background and experiences, a teacher could use other examples such as quilting, instead of using tiles like Rick did, that provide real-world examples of this math concept.

Rick makes time for activities that are not directly related to the curriculum because for SLIFE interconnectedness is a condition for learning. This investment helps SLIFE feel a sense of relevancy to an alien and unfamiliar classroom setting while building their basic literacy and language skills and learning subject matter content. As a result, Rick lessens the sense of cultural dissonance and encourages more positive involvement in the class overall.

To combine the processes for learning, Rick structures activities so that the processes from both learning paradigms are integral to his lessons. Rick finds ways to bring in oral language and shared responsibility all the while leading students to be individually accountable for part of the activity and to use their reading and writing skills to complete their work.

Rick: How am I incorporating both shared responsibility and individual accountability?

Rick's problem for the class requires the students to calculate the number of tiles for each room, add up the results, and then tell him how much tile must be ordered for the entire house. In order to accomplish this, the students will solve the problem in three stages, working first in teams, then in larger groups, and finally as a whole class. Because construction tasks are by nature collaborative with various roles students can play, Rick organizes them into teams. Each team selects a room and signs up on the diagram Rick has posted to indicate which room they will calculate. Team 1 chooses to calculate how many small tiles they will need for the bathroom, and Team 2 for the small bedroom. Team 3 chooses to calculate how many large tiles will be needed for the living room, and Team 4 for the large bedroom.

Rick then breaks the problem into three parts:

1. Calculate how many tiles you need for your room.
2. Form a group with the other students who chose a room with small tiles. How many small tiles in total do we need for the house?
   Or
   Form a group with the other students who chose a room with large tiles. How many large tiles in total do we need for the house?
3. What is our final order of small and large tiles for the house?

When this class problem is completed, Rick assigns each student a similar but different problem to solve individually. This time, the students each measure a room in the school. For the new problem, each student decides whether to use small or large tiles. As support, the student can refer to the previous problem and to the steps.

Rick: How am I scaffolding the written word through oral interaction?

To introduce the topic, Rick begins with a short video clip that he found on the internet. He plays it without the sound so that he himself can narrate it to control the language for his SLIFE class. The video demonstrates, step by step, the calculations needed for a building task. Rick pauses the video at selected points, writes key vocabulary and concepts on the board as he says them, and asks the students to repeat them. In this way, he highlights the academic language they will need, such as *determine, dimensions, length, width, convert.* Later, when the lessons continue with problem solving, the students will be prepared to discuss such problems because of this pre-teaching of the vocabulary.

Working together, the students discuss their own problem, using the words on the board that accompanied the video and Rick's voice. In addition, while one student goes through the math problem orally, step by step, another student writes it out for the group. Then another student reads it out loud to the group. When students present their results to the entire class, they explain the problem while pointing to the solution on the board, written out using the key vocabulary and concepts.

To introduce new activities for learning using familiar language and content, Rick designs his lessons to lead students naturally from a highly relevant, real-world problem to the math skills needed to solve it. His application of the elements of Component C of MALP prepares students for the many word problems they will be asked to read and solve in subsequent math courses.

Rick: How am I developing academic ways of thinking? Which decontextualized tasks am I teaching so students can demonstrate mastery? How am I scaffolding these new activities by using familiar language and content?

Rick intends to build ways of academic thinking into his math lessons, avoiding a focus on pure mathematical problem solving, although that, in and of itself, contains academic thinking. He looks to the decontextualized tasks and skills required to develop and show mastery of the math itself, such as using charts and diagrams to locate relevant data. Rick plans to strengthen the mathematical thinking of the SLIFE by first laying the foundation with these tasks.

Rick thinks that the construction project is a great way to introduce and reinforce the concept of steps in problem solving for math and why order is important in getting to the final answer. Rick has decided to teach *sequencing* as the primary new academic way of thinking to focus on in this lesson. Because this concept of fixed step-by-step procedures is new, however, he must introduce and practice it with language and content SLIFE find accessible. Gradually, he can move them toward the more challenging math concepts he must teach them, and the academic language that accompanies these concepts. As in Christina's lesson, students are encouraged to engage in translanguaging as they discuss this new sequencing process in their languages, as well as in English.

Rick has chosen a construction task to provide a context that is familiar. He uses the same language and content for all the problems the students work on rather than create new math problems, each of which provides a new situation with new content and vocabulary. While the linguistic complexity of math problems poses challenges for all ELs (Martinello, 2008), this is even more true for SLIFE. Rick's use of the same language and content enables the students to focus on the academic thinking they need to engage in and not be distracted by unfamiliar language and content.

Rick shows a video but uses his own familiar voice and language to present it. Rick also writes key concepts on the board while pausing the video. Later in the lesson, Rick provides sentence frames to guide the students in producing their own language about the problem. Each of these techniques makes the academic ways of thinking and the decontextualized tasks he is introducing more accessible to his class.

To scaffold the concept of sequencing, Rick provides a clear list of the steps involved, which, especially for SLIFE, makes getting to the outcome of the problem easier and more efficient. To help the students visualize the problem, Rick uses the building materials themselves. He demonstrates how a construction task must follow a certain order.

Rick shows how other math problems they are solving also have a specific order to follow. He gives his students a template similar to the one he used for the construction activity. They then use this template as they work in teams to solve the problems. Because this sequence of problem-solving steps is new, the emphasis is to become familiar with this sequence, talk about it, write about it, and refer to it when they present their solutions to the class.

Template for Solving Math Problems
• Identify the given information.
• Determine what the question is asking.
• Identify the method you will use to solve the problem.
• Check to be sure the numbers you are using in this method can be combined (same units; like terms, etc.).
• Perform the operations one at a time in the correct order.
• Check that your answer makes sense.
• Draw a box around the final answer.

This template includes two items to which Rick must draw students' attention: *Identify the method you will use to solve the problem* and *Check that your answer makes sense*. For the tile problems, the students did not need to be concerned with identifying the method for solving the problem because their teacher had provided it. He points out that in future math work and on tests, they will be working on identifying the method to use for a given problem. Mastering this academic task is essential for their success.

Rick then explains to his class the importance of checking answers to be sure that they make sense. To illustrate, he uses the tile problem. The rooms are measured in meters but the tiles are measured in centimeters. In order to solve the problem, the students must convert all the numbers to the same unit, either centimeters or meters. To reinforce and practice, Rick shows them how ignoring the units will result in an error if the units are not the same. For example, in the kitchen, if they don't convert the room dimensions from meters to centimeters and instead use the numbers 4.4 and 40 for their determination of the number of tiles needed in a row, they would get just over one-tenth of one tile in each row (4.4 divided by 40 = 0.11 tile) and not 11 tiles.

They can easily see that this is an unlikely answer. The importance of always checking an answer to see if it makes sense becomes a principle SLIFE now relate to and understand. They experience for themselves what happens when all numbers are not converted to the same units. In this case, unlike with Christina's lessons, the students are learning to rely on what is intuitive as they verify their results.

We have seen how Rick has worked his way through the MALP Checklist in his math lesson planning. Because he is incorporating the three components of MALP—the conditions, processes, and activities of this mutually adaptive approach—he is able to both support and appropriately challenge his class of SLIFE. The MALP Checklist helps teachers fine-tune their teaching, noting which elements are missing or need to be enhanced. Examine Christina's and Rick's completed MALP Checklists (see Figures 4.3 and 4.4).

Mutually Adaptive Learning Paradigm®
MALP® Teacher Planning Checklist (Christina)

A. Accept Conditions for Learning

A1. I am making this lesson/project immediately relevant to my students' lives.
- ☐ *Current event relevance: Election approaching – event in the news*
- ☐ *Geographic relevance: New York State – their state – is selected for the model poster*
- ☐ *Cultural relevance: A minority candidate is running for president – they are members of a minority group*
- ☐ *Academic relevance: Math class topic is estimating – population numbers can be estimated*

A2. I am helping students develop and maintain interconnectedness with each other.
- ☐ *Teacher and students share personal connections to states selected*
- ☐ *Students talk about candidates and their opinions about the election*
- ☐ *Partners work together to gather information and make their poster*

B. Combine Processes for Learning

B1. I am incorporating both shared responsibility and individual accountability.
- ☐ *Pairs work together to collect required data*
- ☐ *Each member finds extra data for one state*
- ☐ *Pair produces poster with each contributing to the overall result*
- ☐ *Pairs present completed poster but each member discusses one state*

B2. I am scaffolding the written word through oral interaction.
- ☐ *Teacher gives oral explanation of model poster while pointing to written version*
- ☐ *Teacher reads the model sentences aloud*
- ☐ *Students discuss the information they collected as they write it on the poster*
- ☐ *Students discuss the model sentences they are composing together*
- ☐ *Students explain their poster while other students view written version*

C. Target New Activities for Learning

C1. I am teaching students to develop academic ways of thinking.
- ☐ *Comparing and contrasting*
- ☐ *Grasping a counterintuitive concept by breaking down concession statement into individual statements of fact that underlie it*

C2. I am teaching students how to engage in decontextualized tasks to demonstrate their mastery.
- ☐ *Internet searching*
- ☐ *Creating posters*

C3. I am using familiar language and content as scaffolds.
- ☐ *Guiding their internet search by sharing bookmarks for selected sites*
- ☐ *Real-world content about the electoral college and the election scaffolded by maps, population figures, and data collected*

Figure 4.3. Christina's Completed MALP Checklist

Mutually Adaptive Learning Paradigm®
Mutually Adaptive Learning Paradigm® **MALP® Teacher Planning Checklist (Rick)**
A. Accept Conditions for Learning
A1. I am making this lesson/project immediately relevant to students. ☐ *Using a real-world problem from one of the students* ☐ *Linking math to specific skills students can apply where they live or work*
A2. I am helping students develop and maintain interconnectedness. ☐ *Students share experiences with building materials* ☐ *Teacher shares home workshop photos and experiences*
B. Combine Processes for Learning
B1. I am incorporating both shared responsibility and individual accountability. ☐ *Students work together on the first problem calculating the amount of tile* ☐ *Each team is responsible for at least one room of the house for the second problem* ☐ *Teams combine into large groups to add up their results* ☐ *Each student is individually accountable for at least one additional problem*
B2. I am scaffolding the written word through oral interaction. ☐ *Teacher narrates video while taking notes on board* ☐ *Students work out problems aloud while team members write* ☐ *Students read their work out loud while team members read along and check for accuracy* ☐ *Students present results orally to class with visual representation on board*
C. Target New Activities for Learning
C1. I am teaching students to develop academic ways of thinking ☐ *Students focus on the sequence of steps and the importance of a specific order* ☐ *Students consider how operations must have the same units to obtain the correct answer* ☐ *Students learn about checking their answers to see if they make sense*
C2. I am teaching students how to engage in decontextualized tasks to develop and demonstrate mastery. ☐ *Students follow steps using charts* ☐ *Students interpret diagram of house*
C3. I am using familiar language and content as scaffolds. ☐ *Teacher provides video with his own narrative in familiar language and pauses video to write key concepts on board* ☐ *Teacher provides sentence frames to guide the use of language to describe steps of the problem* ☐ *Teacher uses familiar content of a construction activity for all the problems in the project*

Figure 4.4. Rick's Completed MALP Checklist

For Further Exploration

Four teaching snapshots of lessons designed for SLIFE are presented here. Read at least two of these lesson snapshots and then respond to the discussion questions.

Snapshot A: ESL with Ms. Boudreaux
Snapshot B: Living Environment with Ms. Vargas
Snapshot C: U.S. History with Mr. Icoz
Snapshot D: Estimating in Math Class with Ms. Baldini

Discussion questions for the snapshots

1. What did you like about each lesson? Dislike?
2. What do you see as the strengths and weaknesses of each teacher?
3. Give specific examples of as many elements of MALP as you can find in each snapshot.
4. Identify elements of MALP that may be missing in the lesson.
5. Now, using the MALP Teacher Planning Checklist in Figure 4.1, go back and analyze each snapshot. You may find it easier to practice using the Checklist by breaking up your analysis into three parts, based on the components of MALP:
   a. Accept the learning conditions of SLIFE;
   b. Combine the processes from both the SLIFE learning paradigm and that of formal education; and
   c. Target new activities for learning—that is, new academic ways of thinking, and decontextualized tasks, scaffolded by familiar language and content.
6. How did the Checklist help you in identifying which elements were present or missing? Explain.
7. Using the completed Checklist as a guide, provide suggestions for how the teacher could revise the lesson to include the missing elements that you have identified.

Snapshot A: ESL with Ms. Boudreaux

Ms. Boudreaux's class is composed of fifteen students, ranging in age from fifteen to twenty. As the bell rings, the students slowly come into class and find their seats. The room is pleasant, brightly lit from a bank of windows on one side. The desks are arranged in rows, with the teacher's desk in the front, off to the side. Because this is a SLIFE class, Ms. Boudreaux has modified the state English Language Arts curriculum.

After taking attendance, Ms. Boudreaux begins her lesson by telling the students to get out the list of fifteen vocabulary words that she passed out yesterday and that they were to practice for homework. The words were taken from a fairy tale the students had been reading. She pronounces a word and calls on a student to repeat it after her. Ms. Boudreaux corrects the student's pronunciation and then moves on to the next word and another student. After doing this for a few words, Ms. Boudreaux asks the students, "Do you remember what this means?" indicating the next word on the list. When no one responds, she supplies the definition. For one word, *maroon*, Ms. Boudreaux points to a student and says, "Ana, you know this word; what color is this?" Ana looks at her, puzzled. Ms. Boudreaux turns to another student, Raul, and says, "Maybe you can help Ana." Raul points to Ana's sweatshirt and says, "maroon." Ms. Boudreaux praises him and continues as she has with the remaining vocabulary words. After they have gone over all the words, Ms. Boudreaux asks the students to choose any three words, and to write one sentence using each word. To model this, she writes the word *market* on the board and asks, "Who can give me a sentence with this word?" Two students raise their hands; she picks one, Serge, and gives him the chalk. Serge writes, "I like to go to the market." She praises him and then reminds the class that they are supposed to do this on their own with their chosen vocabulary words from the list, repeating her earlier instructions.

Ms. Boudreaux walks around the class as students work on this activity checking their work. She stops at one student's desk, notices he is having problems completing his work, and repeats the instructions to him, "George, you need to pick three words [holding up three fingers] and write a sentence for each word. You need three sentences for three of these words," pointing to the list. Knowing that George is Haitian and assuming that he understands French, Ms. Boudreaux then chooses one of the words, saying, "in French, this word is ... and in French I can write this sentence with it," as she writes her French sentence. "Now you do this in English," she instructs George as she moves to the next student. The bell rings just after Ms. Boudreaux has completed circling around to each student. She tells the class that their homework is to finish their sentences and that she will collect the homework tomorrow. Ms. Boudreaux reminds them that it is important that they study these words because they will be on the test at the end of the week.

Snapshot B: Living Environment with Ms. Vargas

In Ms. Vargas's science class for SLIFE, the students are learning to classify living versus nonliving things. Ms. Vargas reviews her earlier lesson on this topic by projecting a picture of a jungle environment on the interactive whiteboard. She asks the SLIFE to point to some items they recognize and circles one of those items, a bamboo tree, and writes next to it "living" with a colored marker. Ms. Vargas then has the students come to the whiteboard and circle other items that are examples of living things, using the same color marker. Next, she asks students to identify nonliving things on the slide. Ms. Vargas chooses one of these, circles it in a different color maker, and labels it "nonliving." She then has students come up again and circle these items, using the different colored marker.

Hanging on the wall are posters SLIFE created in a previous lesson on living and nonliving things. For living things, there is a list of defining characteristics for each. Ms. Vargas continually refers to this list during the lesson, reminding the SLIFE to think about each characteristic when they decide whether a given item is a living or nonliving thing. When one student becomes confused and identifies a rock as a living thing, another student points to the chart and reminds this student about the characteristics, for example, "No, rocks no breath."

After this review, Ms. Vargas projects a picture of a pond on the interactive whiteboard. She passes out copies of this picture and colored markers to the class. She then asks the students to identify to which group each of the different items in the picture belong, using one color for living and another color for nonliving. In pairs, the students consult with each other to label the items as living or nonliving things, again referring to the student posters, and working together to decide on which color to circle each item. When they have completed the task and showed their work to Ms. Vargas, she instructs the students, "Each person choose one item and say whether it is a living or nonliving thing. Tell your partner at least one reason why it is a living or nonliving thing." After they have finished presenting their work to each other, Ms. Vargas announces that there will be a test the next day with a different picture depicting a mix of items. For the test, they will have to find, circle, and label each item as living or nonliving. They will also have to name the characteristics of living things without reference to the concept poster.

Snapshot C: U.S. History with Mr. Icoz

Just before the bell rings, Mr. Icoz hangs up a large poster of Abraham Lincoln on one wall and tapes two large sheets of blank chart paper to the blackboard. Mr. Icoz begins his social studies class by talking about the poster. He asks questions such as, "Who remembers who this is?" and "What did he do?" After a few minutes, Mr. Icoz points to the charts and tells the students that they are going to put information about Abraham Lincoln on them. The information that goes on the chart first, Mr. Icoz says, is going to be "What I Know" and the information on the second chart, "What I Want to Know." (We will refer to these as the K and the W charts, respectively.) He repeats the phrases as he writes them on the chart paper. He then asks the class what anyone remembers about yesterday's lesson on Abraham Lincoln. Margot shouts out, "I don't know nothing," to which Mr. Icoz responds, "I'm sure if you think, you'll know something about him." Several of the other students are talking to each other in their preferred languages, Spanish and Haitian Creole, about some ideas. Soon Hennrick raises his hand and offers, "He was president of U.S. in 1860." Dadou jumps in and adds, "I see him on the money. He's on twenty dollar bill." At this point Blanca says, "He's on this money, también," and pulls out a penny from her pocket. Mr. Icoz then asks, "Does anyone have a twenty dollar bill? Or how about a five dollar one?" Sergio laughs and says, "We want the money but we got only the penny." Mr. Icoz takes out his wallet, finds two bills, a twenty dollar bill and a five dollar bill, and holds them up asking, "Okay, which bill has Abraham Lincoln on it?" Dadou says, "Oh, oh, I wrong, he's on the five dollar." Mr. Icoz then asks Dadou and Blanca to each give him a sentence about Abraham Lincoln to put on the K chart.

After they give him their sentences and he has written them in correct English, Mr. Icoz reads each sentence to the class and asks the students what else they can tell him about Abraham Lincoln. Graciela offers, "He is a white man but he help the black people freedom"; Jean, "He killed by bad man"; and David, "He against the slavery." Mr. Icoz continues this activity until the students have come up with ten sentences. He then turns the students' attention to the W chart and asks them what they would like to know about Abraham Lincoln. Victor says he wants to know, "Where he born"; Margot, "How did he became president"; and Hennrick, "How he free the black people." Mr. Icoz again writes all their sentences on the W chart and reads each one back to the class. He has the students break into groups of three and instructs them to come up with at least three additional sentences for the W chart. As the students work in their groups, Mr. Icoz circulates, checking to see that they are on track with the assignment. Once they have finished, he asks them to read their sentences aloud, writes them on the W chart, and reviews them again. When the bell rings, Mr. Icoz tells the class that tomorrow they will review these charts and begin working on a biography of Abraham Lincoln.

Snapshot D: Estimating in Math Class with Ms. Baldini

Ms. Baldini begins today's lesson by passing out a worksheet. She points out the title, "sums and differences," to the students and says, "We're going to be connecting today's lesson with what we learned before about addition and subtraction. On this worksheet we see drawings of articles, such as a handbag and a T-shirt, with prices listed below each item." Ms. Baldini calls on one student, Emmanuel, to read the first few items on the worksheet with the associated prices. She next calls on Lu to read more of the items, then another student, until the class has read through all the items and prices. When a student stumbles over the pronunciation of an item, Ms. Baldini pronounces it and asks everyone to repeat it after her.

Ms. Baldini draws the students' attention to the fact that the items and their prices are listed from left to right, rather than from top to bottom, as is more common in math problems. At several points Ms. Baldini injects humor into the lesson by pointing out the oddities in some of the prices. A blouse, for instance, costs only $14.00, but a roll of tape is $5.00.

When the class has finished reading the items and prices out loud, Ms. Baldini reminds the students of their previous lesson on estimating. She reviews the estimating process by picking the first two items and prices on the worksheet and estimating, or rounding off, these numbers for the students. For example, for a $6.98 pair of socks, Ms. Baldini says it costs roughly $7.00. To make sure they remember the estimating process, Ms. Baldini has the class work with her on estimating the next two prices. When she asks for a volunteer to lead the review on estimating with her, Emmanuel immediately raises his hand. The rest of the class watches quietly while Ms. Baldini and Emmanuel round off, either by rounding up or rounding down, the next two prices. When they have finished the review, she instructs the students to round off all the next five items on their own.

Once the students have completed these five, Ms. Baldini reviews their work by calling on different students to provide their answers. For each response, she repeats the estimating process for that question. When Donni makes a mistake, Ms. Baldini writes the numbers as she reviews the estimating process, step by step, prompting Donni to produce the correct answer. At the end of the class Ms. Baldini assigns the remaining questions for homework.

Part Two

5. Using Projects with MALP

In Chapter 4, we explored how teachers can apply the MALP approach in their instruction by incorporating the elements of MALP into their lessons, as Christina did in her social studies class and Rick, in his mathematics class. As we saw, MALP can be infused into curriculum units as an approach to teaching that is culturally responsive and sustaining. However, teachers can also use MALP as the framework for designing class projects as a supplement to support the curriculum. In MALP projects, teachers target specific academic ways of thinking with explicit instruction incorporating familiar language and content. In this chapter, we explore projects from a MALP perspective and describe one project, the Mystery Bag Project, in detail.

When we consider projects from the MALP perspective, a project may be as basic as producing a summary poster of key concepts on a given topic, or it could take the form of a more extensive one, such as a periodic newsletter. The time frame for projects can range from one or two lessons to several months, or even expand into a year-long recurring activity.

In thinking about projects for SLIFE, we need to remember that these students are in the process of building their identities as learners. While SLIFE tend to be members of collectivistic cultures with a focus on shared responsibility, they may not know how to engage in cooperative learning classroom-style. This includes learning how to work collaboratively, whereby students are assigned specific roles or duties, and learning how to stay on task and follow a set timeline with specific steps. Thus, we want to begin by engaging them in short, simple projects as they become familiar with basic project school routines, gradually increasing their complexity and duration.

Creating and implementing MALP projects can have many benefits for SLIFE. As SLIFE develop familiarity with decontextualized tasks and associated academic ways of thinking through MALP projects, they are also increasing their skills in language and reading and writing. Including and integrating all the language domains, i.e., listening, speaking, reading, writing, and viewing, in naturally occurring contexts helps SLIFE become accustomed to functioning in their new learning context. In addition, the MALP projects described in this book lend themselves to an interdisciplinary approach that builds background and develops content knowledge. Finally, projects set the stage for SLIFE to feel a sense of ownership as they work, something that is difficult for them to achieve in more structured lesson formats. In the next section of this chapter we expand upon these benefits and show how they are supported through elements of MALP:

> I don't know how to deal with such a mixed group [of SLIFE]. How do I balance all their different academic needs in one class?
>
> —Rob, ESL teacher, Atlanta, Georgia

A concern of many teachers of SLIFE is the range of abilities of their students and how to meet their needs. By basing MALP instruction on project-based learning, teachers both allow for and accommodate differentiation, as each project consists of a series of tasks and activities that can be geared to a variety of student abilities and interests. For example, a project may encompass tasks ranging from oral (e.g., interviews), to written (e.g., summaries), to visual (e.g., photos), and on to publication (e.g., bulletin board displays). Each student can then engage in those tasks that are most appropriate in terms of ability. In situations where students may need to take on tasks that are beyond their capabilities, students can support or mentor one another, facilitated by the teacher. This learner-centered, differentiated classroom work promotes developing interconnectedness and, by extension, fosters a learning community.

Promoting Learning by Reducing Teacher Talk

Another significant way of increasing learner-centeredness through projects is by the reduction of teacher talk. SLIFE frequently have difficulty paying attention when the teacher is interacting with one student because they are not necessarily aware that teachers expect them to be active listeners—to listen and learn from the interaction even if they are not part of that interaction. Instead, they may simply wait for explicit questions or directions directed to them, so much of the lesson will not be productive learning time for these students. Consider this exchange:

Mr. Harakla: What's the first step to solve number four?
José: See which number is bigger.

Mr. Harakla: Yes, and María, tell us which one.

María: [No response, after a few moments]: What's the question?

In the discussion of oral transmission in Chapter 2, we noted that SLIFE feel most comfortable when they are receiving messages with redundancy built into them. Although Mr. Harakla is trying to build on his exchange with José to include another student, María, he is unsuccessful. Such types of exchanges build on each other in a linear way so that if students miss the one-time input as in this example, they cannot participate. In this interaction, María does not see herself as part of a communicative chain and thus the exchange between teacher and student has to start all over again. To engage María from the beginning, Mr. Harakla could have set the stage by modifying his initiation, using redundancy:

Mr. Harakla: María, we're doing number four; the question is about the first step. José has said we need to find the larger number. My question to you is, which number is larger?

In projects, because the teacher does not dominate, neither does teacher talk. Moreover, built-in redundancy, clarification exchanges between the teacher and a student, and other elements of oral transmission are integral in projects, providing a comfort level that is generally absent in classrooms dominated by teacher talk. Chapter 4 showed how Christina and Rick facilitated learning among their students through the implementation of MALP and projects. Rather than traditional teacher-student question-and-answer patterns, Christina and Rick's lessons encouraged student interaction, either with each other or with them.

In engaging SLIFE in projects, the teacher acts as a facilitator and guide rather than as the repository of knowledge, and peer interaction and support are central, thereby reducing teacher talk. Learning means *doing something,* not merely receiving information and then reproducing it. Instruction is scaffolded so that students are challenged yet able to reach the next level of knowledge. For example, Mrs. Gomez has her students working in pairs to design a poster. They are the ones actively doing the work and engaging in talk to accomplish the assigned task. The purpose is not only to solve a math problem but also to create a written version of the steps in solving this type of problem, along with the reasons for each step. The academic way of thinking practiced here is to provide support by giving reasons:

Steps	Reason
10 – 2(3)	We multiplied because the 2 is outside the parenthesis and the 3 is inside.
10 – 6	We subtracted because there is a minus sign between the 10 and the 6.
4	We made a box for the answer. Solution = 4.

The time spent on the poster is time-on-task that engages the students and solidifies the concept they have been studying as they talk about their work together and practice writing. Mrs. Gomez has provided sentence frames to help them in their writing, and key vocabulary appears on a math word wall so that they can easily find the terms they need. The poster will have colors, designs, and other personalized additions, along with the content. Once the students have finished their posters, Mrs. Gomez puts them up on the wall so that students can refer to them as needed. When that math unit ends, she selects one or two posters to leave up. The sequence repeats for the next unit and by the end of the year, every student has at least one poster remaining up on the wall. The math concept posters are an example of a recursive short-term project since the same format is used for different topics.

Projects and the Elements of MALP

In the following section, we examine each of the MALP elements to see how projects support the MALP approach. As teachers use the projects described in this book or develop MALP projects of their own, they can revisit the MALP Checklist to confirm that all elements are reflected in the project. They can also tweak the project to add or enhance the presence of any of the elements of MALP. It is important to note that projects that include only some of the elements cannot be considered MALP projects. For MALP to be effective, whether in lessons or in projects, all elements of the MALP approach must be present at some point.

Component A: Accept Conditions for Learning

The first element of Component A, *immediate relevance*, is fostered through projects. Because MALP projects are drawn from the interests and needs of students, they are of immediate benefit and relevance and, hence, are highly motivating. As we saw in Chapter 4, Rick's student, Angel, provided the catalyst for a math project with his need and interest in learning to measure and calculate floor space and tiles.

Projects are ideal for SLIFE in that they can capitalize on the pragmatic knowledge students have—their funds of knowledge. In rural communities, children at a young age begin contributing to the family and gain extensive real-world knowledge that can provide the catalyst for subsequent classroom learning. Livestock and agricultural practices, food preparation, home medicinal care, and traditional crafts are excellent resources. In some cases, children who have not had formal schooling develop curriculum-specific skills that can directly transfer to what they will study in school. They develop robust mathematical skills through participation in such economic activities as buying and selling candy or jewelry to help support their families (Saxe, 1998; Taylor, 2012). The children's engagement in bargaining and negotiating prices coincide with specific mathematical operations and can prepare them for academic ways of thinking about those types of calculations in a school setting. With familiar cultural content linked to curriculum content, SLIFE sense *relevance*, the first element of Component A.

While engaging in projects, students help each other by providing assistance, encouragement, and shared interests, often through translanguaging, which, as we noted previously, means allowing them to use any language in their repertoire, including any English they have already learned. Working together serves to develop interconnectedness and a sense of the classroom as a learning community, which meets the second of the two conditions for learning. Teachers as facilitators of projects are also a part of building this learning community. We stress again that SLIFE are more likely to engage in the classroom and achieve academic success when teachers forge relationships with students and connect to them on a personal level rather than acting as somewhat distant authority figures to their students (Andrews, 2016; González & Ayala-Alcantar, 2008). Nevertheless, the sense of interconnectedness between teacher and students does not mean that teachers accept disrespectful and/or disruptive behavior. The teacher is still a person of authority and must be accorded respect.

During project work, the teacher is available and interacts with individual students and groups of students as needed. Although much of this interaction will center on content, there are opportunities for teachers to demonstrate a caring attitude, show interest in the students as people, and demonstrate respect for their knowledge, even when it is not the same as what is generally considered the norm in formal education. The resulting *interconnectedness* in a classroom centered around MALP projects provides SLIFE with the second element of Component A.

Ms. Eckert's environmental science class is an example of a classroom learning community in which both SLIFE conditions for learning are evident. In this class, SLIFE learned about feeding relationships in ecosystems as part of their study of biotic communities, and made diagrams illustrating the network of interactions and relationships of the flow of energy. They began by creating food chains, which are linear depictions of the flow of energy from one organism to the next, such as grass→cow→human. They then put these chains together into a food web. Because Ms. Eckert had previously introduced the concept of compare and contrast for this project, the students were able to describe a food web from their home country and compare it to the one they were learning about in their textbook. Some students came from the same region of the same country and were able to brainstorm together; others worked with students from different countries but similar ecosystems. In this example, we see how Ms. Eckert accepted both conditions of Component A. By having prior knowledge and new knowledge associated with the students' home countries, there was a sense of *relevance* to the standard science curriculum. And, by having the students share information about their own countries, they learned more about each other's backgrounds and strengthened *interconnectedness*.

Component B: Combine Processes for Learning

In implementing Component B of MALP, teachers combine the familiar processes of the learning paradigm of SLIFE, shared responsibility and oral transmission, with the new ones of formal education, individual accountability, and the written word. As discussed in previous chapters, these processes come naturally to students who have age-appropriate commensurate formal education prior to coming to their host countries. For SLIFE who by definition have not been able to participate in such education, projects lead the way to their making the transition to individual accountability and print. Because MALP projects entail interactive, participatory, and collaborative student engagement, much of the project work takes place in groups or in pairs where students continually share ideas and plan tasks together. However, SLIFE need to become individually responsible and accountable for their work; therefore, carefully planned projects include individual contributions. As you will remember, Christina's students *shared responsibility* by working in pairs to gather information and plan their posters on electoral votes and state size. Yet, each student was *individually accountable* for preparing the material for a given state for the poster.

Print is an essential part of any carefully planned project for SLIFE to support their transition from oral transmission to the written word. This transition should occur naturally during a carefully structured project that includes a written component designed for SLIFE to share their work with fellow students and others. Here, literacy is connected to something personally meaningful and significant to the students, motivating them to read and write. In Rick's construction project, oral interaction linked to literacy practice was evident. For instance, Rick wrote notes on the board as he narrated his video;

she

She has a basketball.

Figure 5.1. Deisi's Slide

later the students read their work aloud as others read along and checked for accuracy.

In another class, Mrs. Conti's, the students were learning the English personal pronouns. In a traditional approach, students spend a great deal of their time completing practice worksheets. Mrs. Conti chose a different approach and elected to have the students practice the pronouns through a project. Each student developed a simple slide deck presentation illustrating the English personal pronouns. For SLIFE, using a slide deck, a narrated video, a podcast with captions, or other technology is highly motivating since it encourages their creativity, while avoiding some of the difficulties these students face forming letters when writing by hand.

To scaffold the project, Mrs. Conti provided a template for slide deck presentations. This template consisted of a slide with a blank text box on the upper right, a blank box in the middle, and another blank text box below (See Figure 5.1). In the text box on the upper right, each student typed in one of the English personal pronouns. In the first text box in the middle, the student then typed in a sentence using this pronoun. (The students had previously worked on writing basic English sentences using different pronouns.) In the middle text box, the student placed a picture, photo, or drawing to illustrate each pronoun.

In this slide deck project, *oral transmission* and *print* were consistently combined, as required for the first element of Component B. In the process leading up to the creation of the projects, the students practiced writing and reading their sentences. As they presented their slide decks, they listened to each other and read what each one of them had written on the various slides. The second element of Component B was also evident, combining *shared responsibility* with *individual accountability*. In preparing their individual projects, the students shared responsibility. Students supported each other in learning the basics of preparing slide decks and helped each other find representative pictures, photos, and drawings. Yet, each student was individually accountable for creating a project that reflected personal choices.

Component C: Target New Activities for Learning

A major benefit of projects is the ability of the teacher to embed the tasks and academic ways of thinking throughout the project. To make these new tasks and ways of thinking accessible to the students, teachers embed them in language and content that is familiar to the students from previous work or from their own real-world experience.

Developing academic ways of thinking cannot be taught in isolation but must be practiced and learned in the context of learning content. Willingham (2009) points out that if students are asked questions such as how they might feel about living in a rainforest, they will be able to provide thoughtful and analytic answers only if they have learned what a rainforest is, including information about climate, soil conditions, vegetation, and so on. If students don't have the requisite knowledge about rainforests, their responses are likely to be shallow— for example, "It would be rainy" (p. 37). Engaging in a project designed to build students' understanding of the ecosystem of the rainforest will provide them with the background for answering such questions and builds familiarity with the language and content.

A multitude of resources can be found on the internet that offer lists of tasks associated with each of Bloom's academic ways of thinking (Bloom, 1956; Anderson et al., 2001). (See DeCapua, Marshall & Tang, 2020 for a more extensive discussion and examples.) Teachers will find these tasks helpful in planning instruction for their SLIFE.

In summary, looking at projects from the MALP perspective, we see that they satisfy all the elements of the paradigm. Projects foster interconnectedness by encouraging group work with individual accountability, combine oral and print, and practice decontextualized tasks and associated academic ways of thinking by building on familiar language and content. Projects permit teachers to create meaningful learning, based on meaningful activities within the constraints of delivering the required curriculum, while developing the English language proficiency, content knowledge, and the reading and writing skills of SLIFE.

A Collections Project: The Mystery Bag

This section of the chapter introduces the Collections Project designed to help SLIFE learn the tasks of classifying, comparing and contrasting, and defining. We examine in detail an example of such a project, The Mystery Bag.

An excellent starting point to introduce academic ways of thinking is to create a class collection of items. These items should share some essential characteristic for classification purposes but differ in ways that are not important for classification purposes. Many items lend themselves to collections drawing from different interests and content areas, and do not need to be expensive or elaborate. Teachers can use collections of rocks, seashells, fossils, books, hats, magnets, bottle caps and jar lids, or coins, to name just a few. For example, Ms. Schaefer has a collection of turtle objects—turtles made out of stone, wood, seashells, and straw, of all different colors and sizes, and manufactured in many different countries. Some of these turtles are purely decorative while others are paperweights, staplers, candles, soap, magnets, or have some other practical use. Despite the many differences, these figures are all still recognizably turtles. She will use this collection to develop familiarity with ways of academic thinking.

The Mystery Bag sample project is based on collections and introduces and/ or reinforces three academic ways of thinking: *classification, comparing and contrasting*, and *defining*. In this activity, the teacher introduces the concept of a collection by giving each student a bag with one object inside. Only she knows that each student has an item representing the same type of object, such as Ms. Schaefer's collection of turtles. The students are instructed to examine their object without removing it from the bag so that no one else can see it. The teacher then guides the students through a series of questions about their object. For yes/no questions, the students respond by raising their hands. For the open-ended questions, the students respond orally. After each question, the teacher writes the results on the board. Gradually, as the students see these results, they begin to realize that they all have the same type of object, even though there are many differences. In Ms. Schaefer's class, although the objects in each student's Mystery Bag differ in size, shape, function, material, and so on, they are still all turtles.

Sample Mystery Bag Questions
• What is it?
• Have you ever seen one before?
• Where have you seen it?
• Do you know what it is called in your preferred language or any other language you know?
• What are some words to describe it?
• How does it move?
• How does it sound?
• What do you use it for?

Working through these types of questions helps SLIFE develop an understanding that, despite differences, there is one salient characteristic common to everyone's object. This, they come to see, forms the basis of scientifically-based *classification*.

Once SLIFE have developed a sense of classification, Ms. Schaefer focuses on comparing and contrasting. She has the students remove their objects from their bags and leads them in a discussion of similarities and differences. The students discuss how the turtles are similar and different from each other, in overall appearance, origin, material, function, and so on, listing adjectives and other descriptive words on the board as they come up.

After students have examined the similarities and differences of their objects as a whole class, Ms. Schaefer introduces a more targeted *compare and contrast* task that further reinforces using academic language and academic ways of thinking. Working in pairs, the students prepare to talk about the two turtles they have and how they are similar to or different from each other.

A final step in this project is to practice the concept of *defining*. Defining terms and concepts is a basic component of most classes across the whole curriculum and in every grade level. One of the most common questions asked in classrooms is, "What is X?" or a variation thereof (Cazden, 2001; White, 2011). For low-proficiency ELs including SLIFE, the response to such a question is often either a translation of that word into their native language or an example of the word, rather than a definition. In the case of SLIFE, it has been our experience that there are two major contributors to such responses. First, SLIFE, like other ELs, lack strong English language skills. Second, and more significantly, SLIFE have not fully developed academic ways of thinking. For these students, such a question makes little sense because defining something based on abstract categories or concepts is an unfamiliar decontextualized task based on an academic way of thinking. The Mystery Bag Project introduces SLIFE to the act of defining by first teaching them about classifications and salient characteristics (DeCapua & Marshall, 2020).

To develop their academic language proficiency and academic ways of thinking, SLIFE need to practice providing more than one-word definitions. To scaffold the task, the teacher provides sentence frames that are commonly used for simple definitions.

As a class and with the teacher's help, students produce a few definitions. In defining turtles, Ms. Schaefer's class came up with the following definitions. Most of their descriptions are based on simple observation, e.g., hard shell, four legs. To support her students in describing the actions of "swimming" and "crawling," Ms. Schaefer showed the class a video. Because the categorization of a turtle as a reptile requires not only an understanding of classification but also prior knowledge of the concept of "reptile," she supplied the term and gave the students other examples of reptiles, building a new schema for them.

A <u>turtle</u> is a <u>reptile</u> that has a <u>hard shell</u>.
A <u>turtle</u> is a <u>reptile</u> with a <u>hard shell</u>, <u>four legs</u>, and a <u>tail</u>. A <u>turtle</u> is a <u>reptile</u> that <u>swims</u>.

Students used these sentence frames:

*A/an*_____ (*the object*) is a/an_____(the category) that has_____.

A_____(*the object*) is a/an_____ (*the category*) with _____.

A_____ (*the object*) is a/an_____ (*the category*) that (*verb*) _____.

This type of guided sentence practice gives SLIFE the theoretical underpinnings of defining so that they move beyond copying or memorizing a sentence from a dictionary or glossary. The teacher can close the activity by having SLIFE practice defining other vocabulary words, either ones chosen by the teacher or suggested by the students.

While a collections project such as The Mystery Bag is especially suited to science classes, it can be used with other content areas as well. What is most important is that students develop classification, compare and contrast, and defining skills—skills that they need in all content area classes. (See DeCapua & Marshall, 2020 for an extensive description of another collections project.)

Projects and the Curriculum

Given the need to cover the curriculum, usually according to a fixed time-frame, teachers may feel that projects will detract from the scope and sequence they need to follow. In fact, just the opposite is true. Projects encourage the integration and synthesis of interdisciplinary content knowledge. It is during project activities that teachers can pinpoint areas of the curriculum that students need to "fill in" in order to be ready for grade-level subject matter in the various disciplines. In this sense, the SLIFE teacher needs to be knowledgeable about the overall curriculum that SLIFE will be navigating.

In order to coordinate and collaborate with other teachers, there are three options for integrating MALP with the curriculum. First, MALP projects can be used to precede a unit in a content area in order to build skills in advance that will be needed in the unit. For example, before a unit on the concept of buoyancy in a science class, SLIFE can do an activity targeting cause and effect in their language class. One way to introduce the concept of cause and effect would be to have students talk about missing school, which is the effect, and the cause, which would be their reasons for staying home. In this case, the effect is the same, but the causes are different. They could also look at a situation in which there are multiple effects resulting from a single cause. Immigration to their new country would be the cause of many changes in their lives that only happened because they have left their home country. Once the concept of cause and effect is internalized, then the students could begin to apply it to the new content they are studying.

Then, to prepare for a lab report on buoyancy, they could work on setting up a step-by-step procedure. In both cases, the content would be based on their lived experiences—not on the abstract, decontextualized concept of buoyancy. What is new would be the formal schemata: cause and effect analysis and procedural sequencing. Once in their science class, they would be ready to learn the new concept governing which objects will sink and which will float, as well as primed to learn the steps in writing a lab report.

A second option for integrating MALP projects is to place them at the end of a unit to give students the opportunity to investigate the content more deeply and develop mastery of the types of decontextualized tasks and academic ways of thinking that are associated with the unit. Together with their teacher, they can review the unit by creating a project that takes the now familiar material and refashions it, such as a class book or podcast. If the topic is buoyancy, they might make a video of their experience with testing a range of objects, narrate it, and make captions for it, showing what they learned.

Finally, as a third option for MALP projects, MALP becomes infused into the sequence of lessons in a given unit, as we saw with Christina and Rick in Chapter 4. While pre-teaching and reviewing are optimal given the need to introduce and subsequently reinforce academic ways of thinking and their associated decontextualized tasks, there are situations in which SLIFE are not taught separately, so that MALP projects must be woven into the curriculum as it is taught. In this case, the teacher can prepare projects to conduct before and after each unit, pairing SLIFE with other students to introduce the specific academic way of thinking that will be needed and then to review the concepts. Translanguaging can also play a role here, but teachers need to ensure that it is included systematically and intentionally in lessons. These projects strengthen the skills of the other students as well because they become peer instructors. For example, returning to our example of buoyancy, the project could be for the student pairs to choose from a list of ideas generated by the class and show how they are examples of cause and effect, explaining and analyzing them in a format each pair would select. This project could be an activity inserted just before the first lesson on buoyancy. Similarly, at the end of the unit, the pairs could choose a format for reviewing what they learned together.

When teachers regard the curriculum as a departure point rather than as a destination, they are able to work with students on projects that are relevant and meaningful for them. When students engage in class surveys (see Chapter 6), for instance, they can use the information they have gathered for developing graphs (math), writing brief narratives (English language arts), researching more information on what they have found and/or using it as a springboard on related topics (social studies, science), and so on.

Projects also lend themselves to developing content-area specific vocabulary. Mastery of content-area specific vocabulary is closely linked to academic success (Zwiers, 2013). Yet, such vocabulary presents a considerable impediment to SLIFE because of the number of terms needed to understand the various subject areas. Not only do SLIFE need to develop a large vocabulary, but even words with which they may be familiar have additional discipline-specific meanings. In math, for instance, *power* refers to the number of times that an amount is to be multiplied by itself. This is a very different meaning of *power* than what SLIFE would encounter in everyday use, where *power* is associated with control, strength, or influence. A more related meaning is found in social studies where *power* is used to refer to the right or authority of governments or institutions. Nevertheless, there are subtleties of difference that may not be easy for SLIFE to grasp initially. Regarding *power*, students might also make an association with electrical *power*, a more concrete usage of the term, adding to their confusion over the term in mathematics. With projects, vocabulary development and reinforcement is a natural product of the process.

Vocabulary is not learned in isolation, and the recursive nature of projects allows for recycling of essential vocabulary, as well as concepts.

Well-planned and well-conceived projects motivate students to discuss, read, and write about concepts drawn from the curriculum, which can be woven into the projects, permitting integration of knowledge rather than providing only isolated chunks of information. Another advantage of projects is that they allow teachers to develop new knowledge as well as revisit and further develop material previously presented. As in Mrs. Gomez's math poster project, the students can refer to earlier posters when they don't remember concepts already mastered and that are needed as the underpinnings for the current unit. The scaffolding from past to present has been provided by their fellow students and is on display in the classroom.

In a project setting, teachers function as motivators, facilitators, and instructors. As motivators, they construct joint projects with the students, helping students identify topics of interest. As facilitators, they ensure that students know what they are supposed to do and when, and they provide essential content and language knowledge. As instructors, they carefully develop learning outcomes based on the curriculum, the needs and abilities of the students, and the topic of the project.

Embracing Technology in Project Design

Another way to support SLIFE is through the affordances of technology. Digital applications provide multimodal options and interactive spaces for robust learning. Teachers sometimes feel that because school is so challenging for SLIFE, it would be a mistake to add technology into the mix; however, the reverse is actually the case. We have observed many SLIFE classes in which the students see the possibilities of using technological tools for their projects and embrace them. Digital-age skills, such as creating slide decks or recording short videos, enhance student engagement. The use of technology becomes part of a project, so the students naturally share expertise and find ways to problem solve for each other. The interactions build community as well as digital skills and the language and content included in the project become embedded as students prepare written versions of their work.

In our digital age, technology develops rapidly, and the specific tools and applications constantly change as new possibilities emerge. Virtual reality has become common in many learning contexts and advances in artificial intelligence will no doubt alter the instructional landscape. In discussing MALP projects, we emphasize that teachers of SLIFE can embrace these new technologies and use them in the service of their learning objectives. Any multimodal solution can enhance learning when used as a support or scaffold to the language, content, and academic ways of thinking being addressed in the classroom.

Here we introduce one such technological tool that has become popular in both school and non-school settings: podcasting. Podcasts are a valuable digital tool for teachers of SLIFE, primarily because they leverage the oral skills of SLIFE.

Let's look at how Yasmeen designed a podcasting project for her students that focused on both their listening skills and their speaking skills, while introducing them to a series of decontextualized vocabulary tasks.

Yasmeen's Podcasting Project

Yasmeen wanted to find a way for students to collaborate effectively on recording a conversation or solo podcast. To provide incentive and reduce possible anxiety around recording, student podcasts from previous classes were available on the class website as models to give students ideas about how to create their own podcasts.

Yasmeen's learning objectives included the following: Students will be able to (1) orally share the main ideas of a podcast designed for English learners that they had listened to; (2) guess the meaning of new vocabulary from context; (3) complete fill-in-the-blank vocabulary tasks using word banks; (4) complete matching activities for idiomatic expressions; and (5) develop and deliver an original podcast on a new topic with support, as well as on a topic familiar to them.

Students listened to the assigned podcast outside of class in preparation for the lesson, going at their own pace and listening as often as needed. At the beginning of class, students discussed the podcasts and talked about the meaning of the new vocabulary in the context of the podcasts, using their entire repertoires of language. Students also responded to comprehension questions that Yasmeen delivered orally. In groups, students co-created a conversation using the new vocabulary on the same topic as the original podcast, but in a new context, and then presented their dialogues orally to the class. The teacher or, when possible, the students, wrote the conversations down to preserve them. Next, the students, either individually or in pairs, produced an original podcast on the same topic using the new vocabulary. Later, Yasmeen assessed students on their vocabulary retention through a series of exercises, such as using vocabulary in original sentences and matching vocabulary to definitions. As a final activity, students individually produced an original podcast on a topic of their choosing.

Yasmeen selected an easy-to-use podcasting application, provided access to an instructor-designed website, created an online space for posting assignments, and an interactive student space where the class could provide peer feedback and collaborate on written conversations.

Elements of MALP in Yasmeen's Project

We see the elements of MALP throughout this project. The topics for this project were all relevant to aspects of students' lives, such as health and education. When students discussed the contents of the podcasts, they related the topics to their lives, thereby sharing personal experiences and viewpoints, and building interconnectedness with each other. Students produced collaborative podcast recordings, working together to produce authentic output in response to the assigned exercises and the written conversations. The activities were structured so that each group member had to contribute to the group product. During performances of the co-created conversations, each student was held accountable for a portion of the oral presentations. The conversations were written down, read, and used as resources, thus combining the oral with the written. Students practiced such decontextualized tasks as completing fill-in-the-blank exercises, and matching words and expressions with definitions. They also learned how to summarize the content from podcasts, first orally and then in writing, thus developing their skill in this academic way of thinking.

Yasmeen's podcasting project provides just one example of how technology can be used effectively in the context of a MALP project. As we discuss additional projects in subsequent chapters, remember that all of them can include technology as an enhancement and support, which often has a positive effect on both student engagement and mastery (Ross, 2020).

Summary

Key Characteristics of MALP Projects
• Instruction is learner-centered, and teachers act as facilitators, advisors, and guides.
• The classroom is dynamic and fluid, with group configurations changing in response to tasks, student abilities, and interests.
• Project ideas develop from student interests and needs but are based on or provide a ramp into required curriculum.
• Projects are recursive.
• Tasks allow for differentiated learning.
• The focus is on teaching decontextualized tasks and associated academic ways of thinking building on familiar language and content.

This chapter has introduced class projects as a way to implement MALP effectively with SLIFE. Teachers intending to integrate MALP projects into their instruction for SLIFE should regard engaging in projects as a major organizing principle. Like any effective instruction, projects must be carefully planned and structured. The goals and objectives must be clear, and the instruction must be purposeful.

MALP projects can be implemented with any level of language proficiency and reading and writing ability, if they are appropriately scaffolded and supported. What is important to keep in mind with respect to MALP projects is that in addition to focusing on the traditional areas of language and content, the goal of teachers of SLIFE should be to build new schemata for unfamiliar ways of thinking.

In the next chapter, we turn to another prototypical MALP Project: Class Surveys. As you read that chapter, notice how the process of designing, conducting, and reporting on a survey illustrates a MALP project.

For Further Exploration

1. Think back to your own learning experiences. Did you ever engage in projects at any time during your schooling? If yes, what was your reaction? What do you remember about them versus individual lessons?

2. Interview at least three teachers and ask them how they feel about having their students engage in projects. What do they see as the pros and cons? How might you address any concerns they express?

3. Look at previous lessons you have taught, or you have observed someone else teach. What projects might you incorporate? Come up with at least two ideas.

4. If you have implemented a project in a class you have taught, try to complete the MALP Checklist (see Appendix A) for this task. What modifications would you need to make it a successful project for SLIFE?

5. Suggest other objects that could form collections for The Mystery Bag project. Think of examples relevant to different content areas, such as math, science, social studies, and English language arts.

6. Sample MALP Project—Class Surveys

This chapter presents a quintessential MALP project, class surveys. By *survey*, we mean any question or set of questions posed to a group of individuals to provide information that can later be presented, summarized, analyzed, and discussed. A survey is a common and very successful language teaching technique, one that is especially appropriate for SLIFE and can become a regular part of the class and routine throughout the year. This chapter examines surveys in detail to show how SLIFE have created, conducted, analyzed, and reported on surveys and how their work exemplifies the implementation of MALP.

Why Class Surveys?

Surveys are uniquely suited to the backgrounds and needs of SLIFE. In fact, we believe that surveys may constitute the single most valuable activity for SLIFE as they transition to formal education and literacy. The steps involved in the survey project incorporate the conditions, processes, and activities necessary for a mutually adaptive approach to the instruction of SLIFE.

- Conditions: Both conditions for learning, *immediate relevance* and *interconnectedness*, fit well with the survey project. Students select topics that interest them, and they find out more about each other's interests and opinions by asking the questions of each other. Students provide support and encouragement for each other as they undertake the survey.
- Processes: The processes for learning, *oral transmission* and the *written word*, combine naturally as each step of the survey project provides for both oral and written components. Similarly, *shared responsibility* and *individual accountability* can be delegated for specific tasks so that the teacher can vary these processes for a particular class and a given survey.

- Activities: Surveys are *decontextualized tasks* that can be used to build familiarity with other different types of such tasks. Surveys help develop underlying *academic ways of thinking*, scaffolded by *familiar language and content*. To create a survey, students generate and sequence relevant questions, presenting them in a variety of formats, quantifying the responses, finding patterns, and reporting the results in an organized form. At the same time, the topic and questions come from nonacademic material related to their lives, or material previously studied, so that the schemata are balanced but with an emphasis on the hidden challenge: the formal schemata of decontextualized tasks and academic ways of thinking.

Surveys, as with any type of project, allow for differentiated instruction because students can take on different tasks depending on their interests and abilities. An additional benefit is that almost any material can be incorporated into surveys and adapted to any language proficiency or reading and writing ability of SLIFE. The information gathered in surveys can be used as the basis for any number of lessons in different content areas. Surveys can be conducted many times during the year, building in redundancy so that students become accustomed to this type of project.

In addition to being an excellent way to bring SLIFE toward formal education, surveys are an important part of social discourse in nations such as the U.K., Canada, Australia, and the U.S. Opinion polls and reports appear everywhere, with opportunities to analyze trends and data. Large collections of polls and surveys on a variety of subjects, for example, can be found at the Inter-University consortium for political and social research (ICPSR), and at Cornell University's Institute for Social and Economic Research websites. Much of the factual information in the Western media today is supported by survey data that can be understood by those who have some ability to decode it. Full participation as citizens is enhanced by this ability, and beyond their academic benefit, surveys provide a springboard to more participation in the world at large.

Survey projects can be repeated weekly, monthly, or at intervals that coincide with the curriculum. They can be related to events occurring in the school or in the community that generate interest, or even to issues in the wider world that students raise in class. The level of difficulty of each task can be determined by the topic, by the students' language proficiency, and by their literacy skills. The built-in redundancy ensures that all SLIFE will become familiar with the academic tasks of the survey. The iterative nature of this type of project is what makes it so powerful for building increasingly higher levels of comfort with a variety of decontextualized tasks and associated academic ways of thinking. Because MALP survey projects are iterative over the course of the year, students have opportunities to perform different and increasingly challenging tasks related to each step, as they feel more confident and ready to take on roles requiring higher levels of language proficiency.

The continuous launching of survey projects throughout the year also gives everyone a chance to learn and participate, regardless of attendance, language proficiency level, or other factors that might impede progress or the opportunity to revisit tasks again and again.

The 7 Essential Steps in a Survey Project
Step 1: Select the topic.
Step 2: Create and organize the questions.
Step 3: Conduct the survey.
Step 4: Analyze and quantify the data.
Step 5: Draw conclusions.
Step 6: Report on the survey.
Step 7: Disseminate the results.

Undertaking class surveys entails following a series of seven steps and implementing the tasks in each step in a seamless manner. Each of these seven steps contributes to the overall goals of building the ability of SLIFE to conceptualize academically, use academic language, and perform new academic tasks. The steps move the students smoothly through the process so that they experience firsthand an introduction to academic ways of thinking. Guided by the teacher, the students learn how to develop from start to finish what is essentially a mini-research project.

The long-term goal is for each individual student to perform all seven steps. The teacher begins by modeling and guiding the students as a whole class, step-by-step through the process. The class uses "The 7 Essential Steps in a Survey Project," posted in the classroom as a resource to help remind students of the steps and for them to check where they are in the survey process.

Any of the seven steps in a survey project can be completed by the teacher, the entire class, groups of students, partners, or individual students. These various configurations allow for differentiation based on the abilities and interests of SLIFE. As the students become familiar with the steps of a survey project, a group of students, partners, or even a single student, can be responsible for an entire project. The various steps in the process of creating questions, collecting the data, analyzing the data, and presenting the data can also be easily and flexibly delegated to either groups or individuals, depending on the specific configuration of the class. The important point to keep in mind is that at least some of the tasks, some of the time, require each individual in the class to be separately accountable, facilitating the transition from shared responsibility to individual accountability.

Teachers may wonder how long a survey should be. There is no set number as to how many questions to include on a survey. A beginning survey can have as few as two or three questions; later in the year, there may be much longer surveys. In working with SLIFE on developing survey questions, teachers need to judge a reasonable number by the students' rate of progress, the time available, the language abilities of the students, and other factors. The actual number should be kept flexible so that SLIFE can take ownership of the survey length as well as the topic and questions.

Introducing the Concept of Surveys

An excellent way to introduce the concept of surveys is to start with an informal one in which the teacher asks the students a few questions, has them respond by raising their hands, and tallies their answers on the board. If working digitally, students can respond using an online survey instrument. Once the students have formed an idea of what surveys are, the class is ready to begin its first one.

Mr. Restauro began with a traditional approach to surveys. He introduced surveys to his ESL class of high school SLIFE by asking them what they like to do in their free time. They each contributed ideas, which he listed on the board. Then Mr. Restauro conducted a brief survey. For example, he asked, "Who likes to watch TV?" After the students responded, he wrote the tally on the board and asked another question, "Who likes to listen to music?" noting again the tally on the board, as shown.

Who likes to...?		
Activity	# of People	Total
watch TV?	𝍤𝍤 //	12
listen to music?	///	3
play video games?	𝍤	5
# of students in our class: 12		

After Mr. Restauro finished with the questions, he showed the SLIFE how individual responses are aggregated and totaled to find patterns. Next,

Mr. Restauro asked students why they might want to have this information from a survey. At first, they were not able to tell him, but then someone in the class said, "What kind of music?" and another said, "Hip hop," and so on, which led them to start talking about music groups and styles. He then pointed out that surveys can help them to get to know each other, share ideas, and learn from each other. This was a good start.

Ms. Yanike, on the other hand, chose to use a digital tool and found that her SLIFE enjoy taking surveys online. There exist many applications to choose from, some more basic, as in a simple form to fill out, and some more complex with multiple types of prompts. Ms. Yanike chose a basic online form to explore a topic that came up in class, which was how students spend any free time they may have after school or on non-school days. She showed them how they could create choices or leave the response open. Then they all entered a response and she showed the responses as a pie chart. She asked them to find their response on the chart and also to look at everyone else's. Then, they looked at the numbers and percentages of students who chose each response.

Discovery Activity: MALP and Survey Projects

The description above of Mr. Restauro's and Ms. Yanike's class surveys illustrate what a survey project might look like. The elements of MALP should already be evident, just from this brief outline. Take a moment to re-read this section and find the elements of MALP before moving on.

We now move through the seven steps of a survey, noting the incorporation of the MALP elements: *immediate relevance, interconnectedness;* a combination of both *shared responsibility* and *individual accountability,* and both *oral transmission* and *the written word,* and targeting *decontextualized tasks based on academic ways of thinking* scaffolded by *using familiar language and content.*

Step 1: Select the Topic

The first step is to select a topic for the survey by brainstorming ideas with the students. To align with MALP, topics should have *immediate relevance* to the students. The survey topic can address subjects of interest to the students that have no connection to school, such as personal tastes in food or music. Because the project is designed to accomplish a partial paradigm shift in learning, and its most essential element is to teach the formal schemata of decontextualized tasks and associated academic ways of thinking, the content, although important to the teacher and students, is not the central focus of surveys at this point.

Initially, surveys should address material unrelated to the curriculum, yet of immediate relevance to the students. For example, the survey could treat a topic related to the school. A teacher can use the survey for the SLIFE to become more familiar with the school and the teachers. In this case the topic is close to the students' current experience so they will be able to generate relevant questions. In Mr. Pinella's class, the SLIFE wanted to better understand what teachers and the administrative staff thought about problems new immigrant students faced in their school, and came up with *What is the number one problem for new immigrant students in this school?*

Surveys do not have to be opinion polls. A survey may entail collecting data on facts about the school or its students, such as how many years each teacher has been teaching. Mr. Pinella's SLIFE wanted to know which teachers in their school, if any, spoke their language or, perhaps, had studied it at one time and generated questions such as, *What languages do you speak?* If doing online surveys, the questions can be sent out beyond the school to gather data from other schools and programs. This wider reach helps SLIFE connect with the larger community and begin to see themselves as a part of it.

Once the students have mastered the basics of survey design, they can move on to survey topics drawn from the curriculum. Curriculum-based surveys provide students with the opportunity to continue processing content to which they have already been exposed. For curriculum-based surveys, students decide on content-related topics and questions that interest them. The survey can give SLIFE the opportunity to make the connections between the curriculum and their own lives and satisfy their curiosity about the curriculum. Surveys can draw from a KWL chart. On a KWL chart, each letter represents one of three areas of focus: K=what I already know; W=what I want to learn; and L= what I have learned. Using KWL, teachers first work to activate students' prior knowledge by exploring with them what they already know about a given topic. Next students, working together as a whole class or in small groups, decide what it is they want to learn, which ensures immediate relevance to them. The survey is then constructed to focus on the W portion of the chart.

Alternatively, the survey can directly relate to a unit that the class has already completed, zeroing in on an area the students would like to know more about. For example, at the close of a history unit on immigration, Ms. McKeogh's class of SLIFE developed a survey on that topic. The students had been learning about the many ethnic groups present in the U.S. and some of the issues arising from its diversity. Ms. McKeogh had introduced two contrasting perspectives on this diversity, that of a melting pot versus that of a stew or a salad bowl. In the melting pot perspective, immigrants become assimilated or merged into the dominant culture, whereas in the stew or salad bowl prospective immigrants become integrated while retaining their unique cultural aspects. The students decided to include a question on this in their survey, "Which is best: melting pot or stew?" The topic was related directly to the curriculum and yet was also immediately relevant to the students. Another question the students generated was related to their home culture, "What one thing do you keep from your culture?" "What one thing do you change?"

Although the class can develop a survey project about any topic, there are some guidelines to follow. Topics should be age-appropriate and should take into account that some issues might be sensitive for SLIFE, given the likelihood that they have experienced trauma and/or may be confronting obstacles related to their immigration status. When Ms. Cicero's class conducted a survey about crossing the Mekong River from Laos to Thailand, she made sure that the all-adult class felt comfortable talking, writing, and generally sharing stories about that journey (see DeCapua, Marshall & Tang, 2020 for a detailed account of that survey).

Teachers will also want to steer students away from topics that may be of interest but would involve more resources and more time than is feasible, so as not to discourage SLIFE who are new to data collection. For example, if the SLIFE wanted to survey opinions regarding climate change, teachers might suggest they limit their survey to an opinion poll of one issue of particular concern, such as the increase in severe weather events globally. Nevertheless, there remains a wide range of possible directions the class could take in designing surveys that promote language and reading and writing skills, develop familiarity with decontextualized tasks and academic ways of thinking, and mitigate the sense of cultural dissonance SLIFE experience.

Step 2: Create and Organize the Questions

Once the topic is selected, the next task is to create the survey questions. The students, working with the teacher, develop a set of questions. The entire class can generate questions together, groups or partners can work together to produce the questions, or individual students can design the entire survey. A survey can be divided into sections so that some questions are group generated and others individually generated. Surveys provide many opportunities to move SLIFE gradually from *oral transmission* to the *written word*. Teachers can begin with a totally or partially oral survey, accompanied by pictures or icons, and with only a few questions. An original introductory survey, for instance, might look like this:

Who Likes to ...?		
	Yes	No

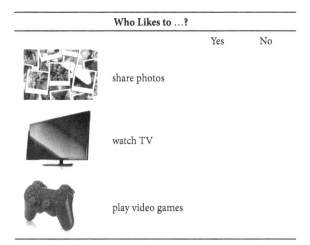

share photos

watch TV

play video games

A survey such as this can easily be administered orally, with the pictures serving as memory prompts for the person gathering the information. Including the labels next to the picture reinforces the written form of the vocabulary items. After students ask each question, they can add a mark under the yes or no column. Once SLIFE become more comfortable using such surveys and extracting meaning from pictures, surveys can be administered primarily in written form.

Given the growing presence of technology in education today, the class is likely to adopt a digital approach to surveys. Some of them help to clarify the material by showing the data in visually appealing formats, such as colorful pie charts. For a more basic approach that also is versatile, the class can use Google Forms. Incorporating technology into the survey project allows students to generate and present data in a streamlined form that can readily be shared widely. Classes can even compare results to those of students from previous years who conducted the same survey.

Surveys provide ways for SLIFE to interact with each other, which helps to promote interconnectedness among students and with the teacher. As they discuss possible survey questions and sequence them, students continually confer with one another. The topics themselves can be selected in such a way that they increase students' knowledge of each other. A personal opinion question can be included in each survey, such as, "What do you like best about our school?"

These kinds of questions help SLIFE become more at ease in the school and build interconnectedness as they get to know different teachers and administrative staff, not only their own teachers. The question, which can also be asked of other students in the school, is immediately relevant as they are getting to know the school better each day.

To identify possible questions for the survey, students will use two main strategies. First, SLIFE consider their own information gaps. That is, how can they use the survey to find out more information about something to which they have already been exposed, but about which they would like to expand their knowledge, as discussed earlier with the KWL technique to create curriculum-based surveys. This is evident in Ms. McKeogh's unit on social media. Students were regularly using various social media and they had been reading about its possible negative effects. They decided to create related questions such as, "Why do you use social media?" "How do we balance the advantages and disadvantages of social media?" "If we decide to leave social media, will we be excluded from society?"

The second strategy is for students to identify issues related to the topic of the survey about which respondents may have different points of view. Students can brainstorm to create questions about such issues, engaging in translanguaging as appropriate. In the issue question that follows, also relating to the study of immigration, the SLIFE wanted to see how others in their school felt about diversity, and they asked, "Do you like the diversity in our school?"

Types of Survey Questions

Survey questions can take many forms. In open-ended questions, the survey participants use their own words to respond, and answers may range from a paragraph or two to just a few words. Open-ended questions allow participants the opportunity to construct their responses freely. Such questions ask participants to contribute their own ideas to the survey topic, for example, or to give a viewpoint on a related issue not covered in the survey questions, as for example:

> *What do you like about living here?*
> *What do you like about our school? Why do you like _____?*

Open-ended questions may generate responses that SLIFE find cumbersome to sort out and could include complex language difficult for them to understand. Nevertheless, teachers may want to encourage the students to explore a particular topic by including some open-ended questions along with the close-ended ones.

In close-ended questions, the responses are provided and the participants select from them. For SLIFE, close-ended questions are generally easier to analyze and report, as the responses fall into predictable patterns, both in terms of language and content. Close-ended questions include five major types: numerical, categorical, multiple choice, scaled, and ranked. Numerical close-ended questions are generally straightforward and answered with a number, e.g., "How many sisters do you have?"

A second type of close-ended question is those that offer respondents choices, one of which applies to them:

Are you
_____ *a student?*
_____ *an administrator?*
_____ *a teacher?*
_____ *a staff member?*
_____ *other?*

Multiple choice questions, a third type, ask respondents to select one or more of the choices, depending on the instructions for the question.

Scaled questions are a fourth type that ask respondents to assign a numeric value to convey their attitudes or feelings by degree. The most common of these is the Likert scale, in which respondents indicate agreement or disagreement, on a five-point scale: strongly agree, agree, neutral (no opinion), disagree, and strongly disagree. For example, the earlier question about diversity could be rephrased as a scaled question:

I like the diversity in our school. Do you agree with this statement?

Strongly agree   Agree   Neutral   Disagree   Strongly Disagree

Finally, ranked questions require respondents to take a series of items in a random order and put them into a meaningful order based on criteria provided in the survey. In a question on school subjects, students could be asked to rank them numerically, depending on how well they like each subject.

In these five types of close-ended questions, the choices are supplied and respondents are offered explicit and limited options. These types of survey questions generate data that are easily quantifiable based on a tabulation of the results. Students can count the number of participants who selected each choice.

The teacher can start with surveys containing only one or two of these types. These are the very types of questions that these students commonly encounter in school but to which they have had little or no prior exposure. As the survey project is iterative, SLIFE have multiple opportunities to construct questions using these five question formats.

Using Preparation to Promote Skills

As students create questions, teachers work with SLIFE to develop language and thinking skills in several ways. First, the very act of forming questions is a challenging task. Questions provide many opportunities for students to become familiar with and practice the different types of question formation. However, it is essential that teachers carefully scaffold question formation. For more specific information, we refer readers to the many available grammar texts for English learners on the market. DeCapua (2017), for example, is a grammar text for teachers that provides detailed explanations and examples of the different question formation patterns that all ELs need to learn.

Second, the teacher and the students ensure that all questions are related to the chosen topic of the survey. Using the list of questions that the class has generated, the students consider carefully which ones really belong in the survey. Evaluating whether questions are relevant or irrelevant to a given topic is an academic way of thinking. Since the SLIFE are new to this way of thinking, they may suggest questions that would be considered irrelevant from an academic viewpoint. For example, in the initial discussion of appropriate questions for the climate change survey, one student suggested asking, "Do you like the rain?"

Third, surveys help to develop the academic distinction between objectivity and subjectivity. Objective questions ask participants for general knowledge or personal information. Subjective questions can be stated as choices, preferences, predictions, or any number of other perspectives on the topic. Surveys can ask for information or opinions, or include a combination of both types of questions, as long as students clearly understand the role of each type and ensure that they are related to the survey topic.

Finally, surveys lend themselves to developing the academic task of sequencing. Once the students have decided on the final list of survey questions, these need to be placed in some kind of logical order. It is important that there be attention paid to the sequence and that the questions not be listed randomly. The students need to learn that general questions should come before specific ones based on the initial general question. A question such as, "How many brothers and sisters do you have?" needs to come before "How old are they?" As teachers develop surveys with their SLIFE, they will find additional ways to use this type of project to build and enhance academic skills.

Step 3: Conduct the Survey

Once the SLIFE have created and sequenced the questions, it is time to prepare the survey instrument. This instrument can be administered in many forms. It can be oral or written, presented nonverbally or verbally, as hard copy or electronically, in English or in another language, or in more than one language. This is one way that SLIFE can become creative and use their nonacademic and nonlinguistic abilities and backgrounds to generate an appealing interface for the participants.

There are several ways oral surveys can be conducted. One possibility is to provide each participant with the written survey, or project it onto their tablets or other screens. The teacher or a student reads each question out loud as the participants read along and respond to the questions on the handout one by one. Another possibility for participants who are less comfortable with print is to provide only the response options on a handout or projected on a screen while the student states the questions. A third option is to conduct the survey completely orally. In this case, the participants hear the questions and respond orally while the person conducting the survey both asks the questions and records the responses.

In preparing an oral survey, students and the teacher will want to consider carefully how students will record the data to ensure later access. Students can record the responses on a spreadsheet or other data-based digital tool designed for analysis and visual representation of results.

Surveys in written form are distributed to participants to read themselves, either on a screen or as hard copy. They then enter their responses, or, alternatively, can give oral responses that are recorded for them. The main advantage of using digital tools for the survey project is that all data is immediately accessible electronically for tabulation and analysis. Nonetheless, in some situations, teachers may still elect to hand out the questions and collect them, as in a traditional classroom exercise. Or, students may pass out their questionnaires to others, such as students or teachers not in their class, school support staff, or community members. When students give out printed surveys or conduct electronic surveys, they should also be prepared to explain the directions and how the results will be used.

Step 4: Analyze and Quantify the Data

The next step consists of data analysis—a decontextualized task that includes many types of academic thinking, such as compare and contrast, discovering relationships, categorization, and classification. For SLIFE to be successful in this task, the process requires thoughtful scaffolding. As SLIFE analyze the survey, they consult with one another to help each other and to compare their findings. The language and content pertaining to the survey are familiar to them because they created the questions themselves. Even when some responses, such as open-ended question responses, contain unfamiliar language and content, SLIFE are likely to be able to use the context to interpret them.

Before engaging in an analysis of the survey results, the students need to review all of the responses carefully. If the questions are all close-ended, this is straightforward. On the other hand, if there are open-ended questions, they will need to be read closely with a view to finding a way to interpret or categorize them.

Once the students have reviewed all the responses, they need to tabulate them. First, they need to see how many total responses they have for each question. Next, for each question they count the number of respondents who selected each of the possible answers and log the data. Finally, they express these counts as percentages or fractions of the total. In this example, the students have done this for one question. Note that the percentages add up to 100 percent.

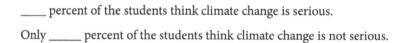

Sample Climate Change Survey Data	
Question	Do you think climate change is a serious global problem?
Results	65% of the students think yes. 12% of the students think no. 23% of the students don't know.

Using the information in this example, Ms. Merimond's SLIFE wrote *More students think climate change is serious than don't.* To help SLIFE in their analysis of data, she provided these sentence frames:

_____ percent of the students think climate change is serious.

Only _____ percent of the students think climate change is not serious.

After SLIFE have examined and analyzed the data, the way that they choose to represent the analysis visually can vary. SLIFE can learn to show their analyses graphically with pie charts, bar graphs, and other such representations of data, which become part of their report on the survey data.

Step 5: Draw Conclusions

Using survey data is effective in helping SLIFE learn to draw conclusions based on evidence. Since by now both the language and the content employed in the survey are familiar to the students, teachers can focus on what it means to draw a conclusion from data. In doing so, the students learn to observe patterns or trends that emerge from the responses. Having a visual representation of the data as in Step 4, assists them in identifying these patterns and drawing conclusions from them. To further develop their academic thinking, students should consider what they learned from the survey about this topic, and how specific questions helped them to get a better understanding of the topic, either in terms of facts, opinions, or both. Looking back at the example from Ms. Merimond's class, SLIFE were able to come up with this conclusion:

> The majority of the class thinks climate change is serious, but about one-quarter are not sure. This means we need to study more about climate change.

Step 6: Report on the Survey

The next two steps require the students to present the results to the class and discuss them, followed by some type of dissemination to a broader audience. The reporting phase mirrors many other such class activities in which presentations are made. In these final two steps of the survey project, the class as a whole will be able to process the material from the survey and focus on the new language and content that may have been generated from it.

As we continually emphasize, sentence frames are an effective way to guide SLIFE in sentence formation. Using teacher-generated sentence frames for reporting results gives SLIFE several ways to present the data they have collected. With such scaffolding, the students can focus on the data they are presenting and yet at the same time build their skills in using the academic language required for school projects. There are many possibilities for students to practice different sentence structures in reporting their results. Here are some examples:

1. The results show that _____.
2. (X number) of people in this survey responded _____.
3. More people think _____ than do not.

The class presentation can take many forms. Students can present the results orally or in writing or both. They can create a slide deck using a presentation application, or they can simply speak about the results and jot down some key points on the board in the classroom, or on a flip chart. The length and complexity of the report will depend on the abilities of the students, but the content of the report is the data. These data will have been tabulated, the patterns that emerged will have been examined, and conclusions drawn. Taken together, the results will demonstrate that the students succeeded both in designing a survey to obtain usable data and in analyzing that data correctly.

As SLIFE hear and/or read the results of the survey, regardless of their individual roles within the survey project, they share the experience of an activity in which the entire class has participated, bringing them closer and building community in the classroom.

Step 7: Disseminate the Results

The culminating activity in the survey project is to show the results of the survey to a larger audience and/or to put them into a lasting format of some kind. In displaying or publishing their work, the students reproduce the material from the survey and revisit it, as in a formal written presentation. The most immediate way to do this is the physical display. This can be as simple as creating a wall poster with the survey results that goes up in the room and can be referred to later as a resource to guide future survey reports and to provide content on the topic of the survey. Another option is to have a bulletin board in a school hallway designated for the surveys and to add them as the year goes along, perhaps with other materials from other MALP projects. Alternatively, posters could be preserved by photocopying and scaling them down to letter size and possibly laminated, for students to keep in a reference binder. The teacher or the students could also take photos of each poster and use them to create an easily accessible reference slide deck. And finally, publishing, as in a newsletter, permits a wider audience. The survey reports can appear on school sites along with other information and/or can be posted elsewhere online. At the conclusion and dissemination of the project, students can share their thoughts about what they learned from going through the survey process.

Summary

Each time the class undertakes a survey project, students may find that they have gained additional knowledge and skills that will transfer to their other school activities. For example, much of the material in subject area classes and textbooks presents data in the same formats as discussed in this chapter. If students have themselves participated in creating such data displays and explaining them to others, they are more likely to understand them and work on interpreting them rather than pass them by or leave it up to others to do the analysis.

It should now be evident how the application of MALP through the survey project helps SLIFE make the learning paradigm shift. A class survey includes all three components of MALP. It accepts the two SLIFE conditions for learning, makes transitions to individual accountability and the written word comfortably, and incorporates decontextualized tasks based on associated academic ways of thinking. Moreover, in this project, students see from start to finish an important characteristic of academic work: the schemata of investigation, analysis, conclusion, and dissemination. After being participants in the entire process, they will be more able to relate to what is presented in their textbooks, by their teachers, and eventually, when they conduct their own research projects, by their fellow students. With MALP as a framework, teachers have an approach they can use to make SLIFE comfortable with formal classroom learning; using class surveys is an excellent place to begin.

In the next chapters we provide multiple examples of projects designed and implemented by MALP-trained instructors, all adhering to the elements of MALP. As readers will note, the projects differ widely in their content and skills focus, and were conducted in a variety of learning contexts with a range of age groups. Keep in mind, however, that these projects can be adapted to any level of language proficiency and reading and writing ability when appropriately scaffolded and supported. MALP is a mutually adaptive approach that combines both SLIFE priorities and those of formal education; therefore, its implementation can be modified to suit any population of students. This chapter has provided a detailed description of each of the seven steps for implementing this prototypical MALP project and we encourage readers to try it out.

For Further Exploration

1. Not all SLIFE feel comfortable with surveys. Imagine that you have just finished introducing the idea of surveys and discussed doing a class survey with your SLIFE. One of the students has not participated very much and looks unhappy. You spend a few minutes alone with him and realize that he feels very uncomfortable asking people questions and thinks it rude.

   a. How might you address his feelings while encouraging him to participate in the survey project?

   b. What accommodations or modifications could you suggest?

2. Properly implemented, a survey project will include all the components and elements of MALP. Since a survey is an ongoing project that takes place over the course of several days, even weeks, not all components and elements will be included in every lesson. Nevertheless, over the course of a survey,

the different elements will all need to be incorporated at some point. To illustrate this point:

a. Reread this chapter.

   As you read, try to fill out the MALP Teacher Planning Checklist with the information provided in the chapter about conducting surveys. You may want to refer back to Chapter 4 and the discussion of the Checklist.

b. After you finish, discuss the following questions with a partner or in small groups:

   • Were you able to provide at least one answer for each of the questions on the Checklist?
   • Was it easy? Difficult? Explain.
   • Which elements of MALP did you see occurring more often? Less often? Why do you think this is so?
   • What additional elaboration of the seven steps for the class survey project would you suggest?

3. Do an internet search for surveys for ELs and find one you could adapt for a SLIFE class survey. Share this survey and discuss how you would adapt it to make it more appropriate for this population.

4. Design a survey activity for your class. Refer to the Checklist to be sure you are implementing all elements of MALP in different steps of the project.

7. Projects from the Field: Young Learners

Beginning with this chapter, we present projects implemented by MALP-trained teachers on a variety of topics and from a range of ages and grade levels. In this chapter there are four projects, all of them designed to introduce young learners to formal education. For children who participate in formal education in their early years, along with learning to read and write, learning about school and building an identity as a learner is a major focus (Tran & Birman, 2017). After this foundational period, the focus shifts to fostering learning skills and developing knowledge mastery at each level of education. It is for this reason that generally students are considered to be SLIFE only after the age of about eight or nine, although there is no consensus as to the precise age for identification purposes (Browder, 2019). Here we share three projects that each target age-appropriate academic ways of thinking. The chart below shows the three projects presented here, along with their titles, the project type, the overarching theme underlying them, and the specific ways of academic thinking targeted in each one.

Project Title	Project Type	Overarching Theme	Targeted Academic Ways of Thinking
The Welcome Book	Class Booklets	Non-Fiction Text	Analyze a Classroom or School Procedure Sequence Steps in a Process
Amazing Animals: Joey the Panda	Data Collection	Research Skills	Identify and Describe Features of an Animal Observe, Collect, and Record Data
Our Lives and the Life of Gandhi	Timelines	Conceptualizing Time	Identify Significant Events Sequence Events Map Historical Time

The first project, the Welcome Book (Marshall & DeCapua, 2010), is an example of how a class of SLIFE can pivot to assist the next group of newcomers by creating an orientation book for them. While doing so, students learn about the structure of non-fiction text and focus on analyzing the everyday school procedures they have come to know. The second project takes students to an online observation tool—a zoo cam—to identify and log the activities of a panda as an ongoing project to translate real-world actions into decontextualized tasks, such as recording and subsequently analyzing their data on the panda. This project builds their basic research skills, such as identifying features and characteristics of a given animal species, and collecting and logging data.

The last project uses a clothesline and clothespins to mark events in the life of an historical figure. This project teaches the class how to conceptualize time through a linear framework, or timeline. While each of these projects could be adapted to different ages, they are discussed here, as implemented by the classroom teacher, with eight to ten-year-olds.

Renee's Welcome Book Project

Non-Fiction Text

Given that SLIFE are new to print-based literacy, one of the main genres they need to learn about is non-fiction text. The features of such a text will be new to them: the table of contents, the chapters, the index, and so on. First, the students need to learn the difference between fiction and non-fiction, and how the latter serves not to tell a story but to teach new information or facts. In alignment with the MALP approach, there needs to be a direct connection to real life and an experience that the entire class shares.

Anything relating to the school is a good place to start in terms of the language and content of a non-fiction book. Although here we describe Renee's project, which she did with young learners, we have seen teachers with SLIFE of all ages engage in similar Welcome Book projects focused on other topics, such as getting around the school or the jobs of different school support staff (see e.g., Marshall & DeCapua, 2010; 2013). Key is that the ideas for such a book are drawn from the students' own school experiences so that the language and content are familiar while they practice the new decontextualized tasks and associated academic ways of thinking.

The typical activity for such shared experience is to conduct a Language Experience Approach (LEA) activity (Van Allen & Allen, 1967). In this approach, an experience the class has participated in together is the point of departure for developing shared text and building literacy. Renee used the LEA as a first activity when modeling what the class would be creating together. To do this, she asked the class what they do when they first arrive in the classroom. Then she wrote what they replied. This continued until they had a series of sentences describing a classroom procedure.

The Welcome Book	Class Booklets	Non-Fiction Text	Analyze a Classroom or School Procedure Sequence Steps in a Process

Description: To learn about the features of non-fiction text, the students create their own non-fiction text by making a Welcome Book for newcomers to their school. In addition to satisfying curriculum requirements, the Welcome Book provides an orientation for the new students who may arrive throughout the year. Such a book clarifies and complements existing school information handbooks and leaflets and, because it is created from the perspective of similar students, provides the most immediate, useful, and accessible information to new arrivals.

Learning Objectives: Students will be able to (1) identify classroom routines; (2) sequence steps in a routine; (3) draw and write the steps of a routine to create a page for the class book.

The Welcome Book

Step 1: Each student produces one page describing a classroom routine that students new to the school need to know: check their folders, use the sink to clean up, line up for lunch, gather on the rug, sharpen a pencil, and rules for behavior.

Step 2: The teacher asks the students about each routine, e.g., *Okay, how do we gather on the rug?* The students chime in describing the appropriate behaviors for gathering on the rug.

Step 3: The teacher then works with the students on sequencing these behaviors and writes them in the correct order for everyone to see.

Step 4: Once students have identified topics for the Welcome Book, they take responsibility for its structure and contents.

Step 5: Together, the class decides which routines to include in the Welcome Book: what other information to add, e.g., a glossary or a map of the school; if and when to use their other language(s) in addition to English; which pictures to incorporate; and what the final format should be, e.g., hard copy and/or digital.

Step 6: Each student is then responsible for creating a page of the Welcome Book that describes one routine. Each page provides a list of steps, along with an appropriate illustration for each one.

Step 7: Each student designs a cover for the book, with a picture of the school and a title.

Step 8: The teacher and the students jointly create an introduction and a table of contents.

Step 9: The teacher makes a class set of the books.

Expansion: The teacher has each student create a photo essay as an autobiography to add to their copy of the book. When new students arrive, they can look through the books to learn about the students in the class and then add their own autobiographies.

Technology Integration: Although this project was completed without technology, it could be easily adapted to digital book creation, as will be discussed in Beth Evans's Wondering About Hedgehogs project in Chapter 8. The individual books, each with its own cover, could still be produced in hard copy to distribute to newcomers.

Katie's Panda Project

Data Collection

In formal education, there is a major emphasis on justifying or proving what one states. Because one of the clearest ways to demonstrate something is to provide directly observed evidence, data collection and reporting is a logical choice for a MALP project. If the data is linked to the real world and to the five senses, then it is more likely for it to be accessible for SLIFE. The project described here is essentially an introduction to research skills. It is also a pathway to learning about the scientific method. Observation was one of the first activities the students undertook. Being able to collect information, organize it, and interpret it are skills that all students need in order to succeed academically, regardless of the subject matter. While sources would ultimately be print-based, a project that uses video as a source is also a good starting point for SLIFE. It is important to keep in mind that here we are focused on the academic mindset, and to make it more effective initially for SLIFE, teachers should avoid relying on dense text.

Amazing Animals: Joey the Panda	Data Collection	Research Skills	Identify and Describe Features of An Animal Observe, Collect and Record Data

Description: To learn about the characteristics of animals that identify them as members of particular species the students get to know one particular animal, Joey the Panda. In addition to satisfying curriculum requirements for animal study, this Joey the Panda project provides a basic introduction to observation, finding patterns in data, and recording information—all essential research skills that will be needed throughout the school years. The students become researchers, in a sense, as they explore and share the daily life of one animal. To prepare them for this exploration, Katie designs a series of steps as building blocks to guide their thinking and heighten their interest in the project.

Learning Objectives: Students will be able to (1) categorize photos of an animal according to science-based features; (2) log data collected through observation; and (3) describe an animal's activities based on analysis of patterns in the data.

Amazing Animals: Joey the Panda

Step 1: The teacher decorates the classroom to reflect the theme of the unit. Students walk around the room and share what they notice.

Step 2: Using photos of panda behaviors, habitats, and daily activities, the teacher introduces the vocabulary orally.

Step 3: Students practice sorting the pictures of pandas into four categories: (1) physical characteristics; (2) habitat; (3) where they live; and (4) what they eat. The content specific vocabulary items are written on white vocabulary cards that correspond to the various panda photos. These cards help them to categorize the photos.

Step 4: Once the students have categorized the photos—an academic way of thinking—they create sentences about pandas. To support this activity, the teacher prepares two additional sets of cards: describing words on red cards and action verbs on green cards. Students have conversations about what they observe and use the different colored word cards as resources to help them make sentences about the photos.

Step 5: Using the Language Experience Approach (LEA), the teacher writes what the students say as they form sentences about each topic based on the photos they have categorized.

Step 6: Students observe Joey, a panda at a local zoo, via a webcam, on a regular, daily basis.

Step 7: Students record Joey's activities on the daily log. The log is displayed on chart paper and titled "What is Joey doing?" Under the title are three columns for the students to log Joey's activities: Date / Time / Activity

Expansion: Conduct a mini-lesson on how to draw a panda. Students watch a video tutorial recorded by an artist that shows students step-by-step how to draw a real-life panda.

Technology Integration: In this project, Katie used the zoo cam to bring students into the world of the panda in real time and in a real zoo. This project was hands-on with hard copy photographs, and flip charts for data collection and sharing, activities that could easily be moved into online spaces so that the entire project is conducted with digital tools.

Judy's Timelines Project

Mapping Time

Because their access to formal education has been limited, SLIFE are frequently unaware of historical events, whether in their own country or in the world at large. Thus, one of the roles of teachers of SLIFE is to develop a sense of linear, historical time. Mapping time is an indispensable concept for SLIFE and focuses their attention on *sequencing*—an academic way of thinking. Timelines can easily be incorporated into many lessons, and they are a very simple, yet effective way of introducing and fostering the sense of time expected in formal education.

We suggest that teachers of SLIFE begin with timelines that show personal information and other events that the students deem important. Personal timelines provide immediate relevance and encourage interconnectedness, as students share their information with each other while developing an academic way of conceptualizing time. Once SLIFE have mastered the concept of timelines, they can be used for many different topics in the curriculum.

Our Lives and the Life of Gandhi	Timelines	Conceptualizing Time	Identify Significant Events Sequence Events Map Historical Time

Description: Judy implemented her MALP project in a language arts and social studies class for her nine- to ten-year-olds. Using the concept of timelines and beginning with familiar language and content, Judy led the students to an understanding of the life of an historical figure, Mahatma Gandhi. Judy began by using an online application for creating a timeline of one's own life. As she told the students about events in her own life and the dates when they took place, Judy placed them one by one onto her timeline. Next, the students made their own personal timelines as a paper and pencil activity. The students then worked with events from Gandhi's life. Based on his storyline from their social studies class that Judy had presented to them, both orally and written, the students hung clothespins with pertinent information about Gandhi attached, to mark events in his life along a clothesline she had hung in the middle of the classroom.

Learning Objectives: Students will be able to (1) create a timeline to depict the order of events in the life of a major historical figure; (2) provide information about the figure based on the timeline; (3) read information about events in the life of an historical figure in a variety of formats; and (4) answer questions in writing from the information in a sequenced timeline about events in the life of an historical figure.

Our Lives and the Life of Gandhi

Step 1: The teacher tells the class about important events in her life.

Step 2: The teacher accesses a digital timeline application and enters her personal information, sharing both the date and the event.

Step 3: Working in pairs, the students share important events in their lives.

Step 4: The students create individual timeline posters of their events.

Step 5: The teacher shares information about Gandhi's life as the class listens and reads the text along with her.

Step 6: The teacher writes events in Gandhi's life on cards, one for each student. Each student chooses one of these events and attaches the card to a clothespin.

Step 7: The teacher strings a clothesline across the room. Students organize their events by attaching their cards with the clothespins to the line in chronological order to create a timeline.

Step 8: The students create sentences about Gandhi's life, talking about the experiences he had before or after certain other events in his life.

Step 9: Each student individually writes a short paragraph about Gandhi's life, selecting events from the clothesline timeline.

Expansion: The students cut up their posters of their life events, and put the events out of order; their partner reorganizes the events and sequences them.

Technology Integration: The teacher used a web-based application to create her model timeline. Another option would be for students to use the same application on individual devices to create their own personal life events timeline. The timeline for Gandhi's life could be created collaboratively using an online tool designed for group sharing of information in a jigsaw-like manner.

Conclusion

These sample projects all incorporate the elements of MALP. After completing one of these projects, teachers may decide to include an additional step, a debriefing of the activity. Integrating a debriefing phase can be very important as it encourages SLIFE to become aware of the specific new ways of academic thinking they have practiced in the activity. Such questions as, "Why did we do this activity?" Or "What new skills did you learn that you can use?" may assist them in making connections to their other schoolwork. They could, for example, simply recall, e.g., "We drew pictures of school; We watched the panda; We made a clothesline." We strongly believe that talking about thinking is as important as the activity itself so that students become accustomed to thoughtfully and purposefully analyzing their thought processes.

These are examples of projects that teachers can adapt and adjust to their own students and their own curriculum. They can also become iterative if teachers want to implement them on their own in different contexts or subject areas. SLIFE benefit from redundancy as they work toward mastering the academic ways of thinking that are manifested in the decontextualized tasks included in these projects. Moreover, as the year progresses, the same projects can be made more complicated and the tasks embedded with more difficult material, further moving SLIFE toward academic success.

The activities on page 150 ask you to reexamine these projects to see how they might be altered or expanded for additional practice. The flexibility of MALP allows for many variations on these projects. The key is to follow the MALP Teacher Planning Checklist to ensure that all elements are included and that the mutually adaptive intent of the three components of this instructional approach is carefully followed.

For Further Exploration

1. Mrs. Aquino decided that by creating a timeline activity focusing on birthdays, she would include cultural information that would enhance the experience of her newly arrived SLIFE. First, she conducted lessons on the months of the year and on the cardinal and ordinal numbers from one to thirty-one. Mrs. Aquino then gave each student a small poster with a template on it that had two sentence frames and had them work with a partner to complete their posters.

   My birthday is on the (_day_) of (_month_). My birthday is (_month_) (_day_).

   Once the students completed the posters, the next step was for the students to arrange themselves physically into a class timeline. Collaboratively, the students examined the posters and arranged themselves in the correct chronological order. When they had finished, Mrs. Aquino told the students her birthday and asked them to indicate where she should stand. Finally, Mrs. Aquino drew a timeline on the board and the students entered their birthdays. Mrs. Aquino summed up the activity by explaining that they had created a timeline, a visual representation of linear time.

   a. Use the MALP Teacher Planning Checklist to find the elements of MALP in this project.

   b. Discuss how you could or could not implement this project with your students.
   - Describe what changes you would make, if any.
   - What follow-ups or extensions can you suggest based on this activity?

2. Calendars are often new for SLIFE, at least in the ways that we use them to mark dates and events, and as reminders to ourselves. Mrs. Aquino, to help her SLIFE become more familiar with calendars and time references, puts a large month-by-month calendar up on the wall, and the students enter their respective birthdays on the appropriate day and month.

   Look back at Judy's project on timelines, using events in a person's life or career to mark places on a clothesline, and think about how that relates to learning about calendars.

   a. Explain how producing a timeline and then a calendar with SLIFE would be scaffolding for Component C of MALP.

   b. What are some other items you could use for a calendar with your class?

3. Consider how you might adapt Katie's project for adolescent learners.

   a. What animal(s) might you have them observe?

   b. How might your objectives differ from Katie's and why?

   c. Explain how your project would fit into the curriculum.

4. Sometimes there is a situation in which there are only a few SLIFE. In Ann's case, there was only Marisa, a student she was assigned at her elementary school, who had no reading and writing skills in any language but who was placed in a class with her peers, all nine years old and reading at grade level, where she was completely lost. Ann worked with Marisa in a tutorial setting, using a dialogue journal to build a relationship and to share experiences in a print-based format to increase her literacy skills. For example, when Ann and her daughter were decorating eggs for Easter, Ann shared photos of the activity with Marisa, along with a short written description of the activity in the journal. Marisa responded by asking if she and Ann could also decorate eggs, take pictures, and write about the experience.

   a. How might you approach a dialogue journal with a student whose reading and writing skills are basic?

   b. How might technology be used to enhance this dialogue journal project?

8. Projects from the Field: Adolescent Learners

Working with teen SLIFE can be a challenge, both affectively and cognitively. In many cases, these students consider themselves to be adults, with jobs and full lives outside of school. In addition, the pressure to complete their schooling within a specified time period can compound the challenges that they face. The projects included here demonstrate how such students can be brought into the instructional setting and helped to develop an academic mindset through relevant connections and meaningful activities for learning.

The three teachers we present in this chapter, Danielle Golub, Lesly Garcia, and Beth Evans, work with adolescent learners who face a difficult dilemma. These students are focused on completing their education, but they may not have enough time to master their new language and the subject matter content required before they are no longer eligible for free public education.

The three projects continue the themes from the previous chapter: an academic perspective on familiar, lived experiences, as in Renee's Welcome Book; an analytical conceptualization of time, as in Judy's Life of Gandhi project; and an introduction to research skills, as in Katie's Joey the Panda project.

Project Title	Project Type	Theme	Targeted Academic Ways of Thinking
Hispanic Heritage	Cultural Perspectives	Lived Experiences	Distinguish Relevant and Irrelevant Compare and Contrast
Time Capsule	Current Events	Conceptualization of Time	Predict Distinguish Fact and Opinion Analyze Significance
Wonderings about Hedgehogs	Class Booklets	Research Skills	Use and Cite Sources Paraphrase Summarize Build Technology Skills

Danielle's Hispanic Heritage Project

The first teacher, Danielle, has students focus on what makes their culture unique and on identifying specific products, practices, and perspectives that distinguish it from other cultures. In Danielle's project, as in Renee's in the previous chapter, the students are already familiar with the material and are learning to organize it and share it in new, academic ways. In this particular class, all of the students come from Latin American backgrounds, although they do not all come from the same country, speak the same dialect or even language, or share the same culture. Many of the students have not reflected on their cultures despite these cultures being part of their identity and daily lives. Danielle has found that by analyzing their cultures, comparing and contrasting them, and finding ways to share them with each other, her students can accomplish a great deal academically, as well as deepen their interconnectedness. This project could be conducted with any mix of cultures.

Hispanic Heritage	Cultural Perspectives	Lived Experiences	Distinguish Relevant and Irrelevant Compare and Contrast

Description: In this MALP project for ages fourteen to fifteen, students explored their own cultural backgrounds, learning more about themselves and sharing this new learning with the other students in the class. In Danielle's class, all of the students came from Hispanic heritage backgrounds but from different cultures. This project opened up opportunities, not only for interconnectedness, but also for a variety of academic ways of thinking. Students were able to notice both what was similar in all of the data they collected and, at the same time, what was different. Moreover, since September was Hispanic Heritage month in the U.S., and the start of the new school year in her state, this MALP heritage project was a wonderful way for the teacher to learn about the new group of students, and to engage them right away in a project relevant to their lives. It was also an opportunity to introduce the students to their district usernames, passwords, and emails and, also to each other, encouraging group cohesion.

Learning Objectives: Students will be able to (1) share information about their culture and heritage orally and in writing; and (2) create a visual representation of their culture and heritage using a graphic presentation application.

Hispanic Heritage

Step 1: The instructor presents a slide deck about herself and her heritage. This serves as a model so that students have an idea of what they will be creating.

Step 2: Students learn how to introduce themselves and ask others for information, using sentence frames to practice. They then meet and greet their classmates, asking for and giving their name and where they are from.

Step 3: After students write down the information they gather, they introduce one of the students from their list.

Step 4: Students watch a video about a young woman cooking with her grandmother. They are discussing the recipe and how it has been passed down through generations. Next, the class brainstorms, using whole group discussion and a partner "turn and talk" opportunity, to come up with other examples of culture/heritage, e.g., religion, clothing, music, dancing, and certain holidays.

Step 5: Students interview family members to create a list of customs special to their family or heritage.

Step 6: Students learn how to use district passwords, usernames and email addresses, and associated vocabulary. They also learn how to use the @ symbol, make capital letters, and so on.

Step 7: Students research landmarks, folktales, and other interesting information they would like to share about themselves, their heritage, or their country. Students save photos from their research to attach to their project. (Teaching them how to cite their sources is also covered.)

Step 8: Students learn how to create a slide deck, e.g., how to select different themes and layouts, experiment with fonts, and import their photos.

Step 9: Students create a slideshow about themselves and their heritage.

Step 10: As students create their slides, the instructor shifts the focus to text and narration, providing feedback. Students practice editing, engaging in both self and peer editing of their projects.

Technology Integration: Students use district computers in order to learn how to use their district emails and log in to district-issued devices. Students learn how to create slide decks, a skill they can apply to future projects in any class. This project can very easily be converted for hybrid/online learning by creating a digital folder where they can post their work and leave comments for fellow students.

Danielle comments: "This project was very fun and engaging for our class, it can also be emotional at times since my students have recently arrived and are often missing members of their family and their homes. This vulnerability really allows me to get to know my students, and for them to learn about me. Students also learn a lot about their peers in the process, and they are able to make connections amongst themselves, their cultures and journey."

Lesly's Time Capsule Project: The Effects of COVID in My Community

The next teacher we describe in this chapter is working with eleven-year-olds on thinking analytically about time. Unlike the previous project about time-lines in Chapter 7, in this time capsule project students will be projecting for-ward in time to assess what they believe is most significant about the current moment to share with future generations. Collaboratively, the students gather ideas and make plans for their class time capsule.

Time Capsule	Current Events	Conceptualization of Time	Predict Distinguish Fact and Opinion Analyze Significance

Description: This project was undertaken during a four-week summer school program for newcomers and SLIFE. Since the theme for the summer reading was "Remembering 9/11", students were given texts that focused on that moment in time. The social studies teacher planned a lesson on 9/11 to prepare the students for this project. For this MALP project, SLIFE learned about the effects that major events, such as COVID-19 and 9/11, can have on a community. The focus was to connect past and present events and to reflect on what we all might remember in the future regarding moments in time such as these.

SLIFE were to co-create a text demonstrating the before and after impacts of COVID-19. In math, students worked on looking at data from COVID-19, using mean, median, and mode. In social studies, students reflected on what type of monument they might build to commemorate this event. The effort of ESL, social studies, and math teachers connecting their curriculum made it relevant and meaningful for students. The interdisciplinary approach to developing these final projects allowed for students to be able to make connections across content classes and further understand the depth and impact of major events in the past or present and how they may impact the future.

Learning Objectives: Students will be able to (1) interpret their place in time and the effects moments in time can have in a community; (2) write a personal narrative about a moment in time; and (3) compare and contrast different moments in time.

Prior to participating in this project, Lesly presents students with an *I Am From* poem to talk about memories that illustrate moments in her life, sharing orally with images and then reading the text. The students subsequently created their own *I Am From* poem. Later, they compared and contrasted themselves in pairs using information from their poems. Once the academic way of thinking, comparing and contrasting, became familiar, the students applied this to comparing and contrasting the effects of 9/11 and COVID-19, using photographs and videos.

Time Capsule: The Effects of COVID in My Community

Step 1: The teacher leverages prior knowledge by having students draw or write about events and experiences they remember from growing up in their country, such as foods they ate, sounds or smells they recall, phrases they heard, and so on.

Step 2: Students practice organizing information by filling out a poem template similar to the teacher's model, using the information from their prior lives.

Step 3: Students create their own poems about themselves using the same structure as the teacher's poem, and then share them, along with visuals.

Step 4: Students compare and contrast each other's past experiences in pairs, using information from their respective poems.

Step 5: To build information, students work in groups to look at pictures and watch videos of two moments in time, 9/11 and the COVID-19 lockdown that took place when governments shut everything down in March 2020 in the hope of containing the spread of the virus.

Step 6: Using what they had learned about 9/11 in social studies and their current experiences with COVID-19, students work together to interpret the similarities and differences they see, including the pictures and videos from those two moments in time and filling information into a graphic organizer.

Step 7: Students watch personal 9/11 narratives posted online, as well as videos of their own teachers sharing their memories of this event.

Step 8: The class brainstorms on how school activities were "Before COVID-19" and "After COVID-19." They walk around the school taking pictures of themselves demonstrating the "Before" and "After" ideas they have listed and write a page of a class text focused on capturing the "Before and After" of COVID-19.

Step 9: To practice hypothetical thinking, students create written narratives in response to: "20 years from now, what will be one moment during the pandemic that you will remember?" They need to think of what their future selves will remember about the present event (COVID-19), similar to what people (like their teachers) still remember about the events of 9/11. Students present a collection of their narratives as a book to peers and teachers in the form of a Time Capsule.

Expansion: Students explore interactive timelines using the New York City 9/11 museum website.

Technology Integration: Students use online shared documents, slide decks, and translation tools, as well as access online resources such as 9/11 interactive timelines from the New York City 9/11 memorial website and YouTube videos.

Lesly comments: "The effort of ESL, social studies and math teachers connecting their curriculum made it relevant and meaningful for students.

The interdisciplinary approach to developing these final projects allowed for students to be able to make connections between content classes and further understand the depth and impact of major events in the past/present and how they may impact the future."

Beth's Wonderings about Hedgehogs Project

In the previous chapter we saw how Renee's project, The Welcome Book, serves to introduce young learners to the concept of non-fiction texts and their basic structure. We also saw how in Katie's Panda Project conducting observations of Joey prepared her young learners to analyze data. In this chapter, the last project we examine is Beth's Wonderings About Hedgehogs in her class with fourteen- to twenty-four-year-old students. (Note: There is no upper age limit for high school in her U.S. state of Vermont.) Here we see how Beth centers the project around building essential research skills, such as using sources to gather information. Unlike Katie's younger learners, however, Beth's students use written sources and learn how to cite them to avoid plagiarism. On the other hand, like Renee's project, Beth's class collaboratively creates a non-fiction text to share. Beth and the school librarian, Shannon, work together to create this digital class book on the students' research on hedgehogs, which is stimulated by the school pet, kept in the library.

Project Title	Project Type:	Overarching Theme:	Use and Cite Sources
Wonderings about Hedgehogs	Class Booklets	Research Skills	Paraphrase Summarize Build Technology Skills

Description: Students collaboratively create and record a digital book, using research skills and science concepts related to the study of animals, such as habitat, diet, behaviors, and the impact of humans on their lives. Otie, the library's pet hedgehog, is the jumping-off point to create this digital "All About" book. Students learn how to research answers to their own questions with credible resources, learn about the library as a source of information, and gain technology and computer literacy skills.

Learning Objectives: Students will be able to: (1) research and answer questions using both print and digital sources; (2) analyze websites to determine reliability of digital resources, including photos; (3) cite sources; (4) restate and summarize information; and (5) use technology to create a digital artifact and to read and record its contents.

Wonderings about Hedgehogs
Step 1: Students observe the hedgehog to gather visible information, list the observations, then sort them into categories, such as habitat. Through a process of shared and interactive writing, using LEA or a similar technique, students compose a paragraph to describe what they notice.
Step 2: As a class, they fill the whiteboard with as many questions or "wonderings" as possible. The librarian answers some of the questions, relying on her personal interactions with the pet. With the teacher's guidance, students narrow the field of questions to those they would like to include in a group book, which they list on chart paper.
Step 3: The teacher and librarian lead the class on a tour of websites to learn how to evaluate sources by working with the students to notice what makes a given site relatively trustworthy. The librarian leads them through a checklist of what to look for to determine legitimacy.
Step 4: Students write their names next to a question that piques their curiosity. To promote successful outcomes, students are guided toward a research question that meets their proficiency level. The teacher creates the slide deck with page numbers, questions, and placeholders for each student's name and photo.
Step 5: To research answers to their questions, students gather in the library to locate resources, both printed materials and digital ones, as well as sites with read-aloud features to support students with developing print-based literacy skills. Using a worksheet, they attempt to find information from two sources and write the answer to the question they choose.
Step 6: The librarian demonstrates how to find information on Creative Commons licensing for photos. The teacher then demonstrates how to add citations to their slides for text and artwork.
Step 7: Students use checklists to evaluate whether the text, citations, and photos are in place to be sure that spelling is accurate and grammar is acceptable for their level of language acquisition. The teacher then uploads the slide deck onto the book creation application.
Step 8: The librarian works with students to add audio. Students read their own pages aloud, first practicing, then recording. Students are afforded multiple opportunities to re-record and give final approval to their page.

Technology Integration: In this project, students learn how to use laptops and applications from the Google Suite. For other projects, teachers can use live zoo cams or YouTube videos to observe other animal activities, such as birds hatching in nests. There are websites with read-aloud resources for students with emergent reading and writing skills and various programs for creating digital books.

Beth comments: "In mainstream classrooms, there is an assumption that students in high school should already know how to create a slide deck, or do research, or cite sources, or even check email. When teaching SLIFE, it's essential to teach what one plans on assessing without assumptions of prior schooling, even if that student has been in U.S. schools for a few years. If that background knowledge is not there, students are condemned to falling behind and appearing as though they 'don't care,' when nothing could be further from the truth."

The project was a class book on hedgehogs that they completed collaboratively. This project prepared them for doing similar types of research and using similar technology skills in any of their subject areas. Throughout this project, Beth was differentiating for her SLIFE in several ways. For example, she gave students a choice of questions, but steered more difficult questions to more advanced learners. Also, she asked others to record for students with speech issues or students who felt uncomfortable or not ready to record themselves. In the end, all the SLIFE were able to participate at their own level and experience success.

Conclusion

As we have seen in the discussion of these three projects in this chapter, as well as The Mystery Bag in Chapter 5, the class surveys in Chapter 6, and the projects for young learners in Chapter 7, MALP Projects designed for SLIFE can be both engaging and challenging, addressing all the elements of MALP and moving SLIFE forward in their journey to success in formal educational settings. (For another good example of a project that addresses all the elements of MALP, see DeCapua & Marshall, 2022 for a description of Yanni's ballroom dance project.) Our hope is that through presenting the projects of actual classroom teachers, as well as outlining templates for MALP projects more broadly, as in Chapter 5, we have provided a number of resources for applying MALP to classrooms where SLIFE are present. These projects can all be implemented in classrooms where other students are also learning together with SLIFE; while they are explicitly designed with MALP in mind, they are not exclusive to SLIFE and can build academic language and content knowledge for all students.

In the next and final chapter, we reflect on MALP, visiting both a teacher and a student who made the journey of MALP discovery and found themselves in a stronger, more confident place in their instruction and their learning, respectively.

For Further Exploration

1. Go back to Chapter 7 and choose one of the projects to adapt for your adolescent SLIFE.
2. Hughes & Greenhough (2006) describe an assignment where students took home an empty shoebox to decorate and fill with objects of personal importance to them. The teacher also filled her own box to provide students with glimpses into her life outside of school and to foster interconnectedness.

The contents of these shoeboxes were used in different subject areas. For math, for instance, the students weighed and measured different objects from their boxes while for English language arts the students wrote about the provenance of the different items.

Reflect on the Shoebox Project:

a. How do you see this project as fitting into the MALP instructional model? Be specific. For example, what decontextualized tasks and associated ways of thinking do you think you could incorporate into such a project?

b. The objects in the box were used in different classes for different lessons. Can you think of how these objects could be used in your subject area?

c. How might this activity be incorporated into Danielle's Hispanic Heritage Project?

3. Consider this project developed by Dr. Anita Bright, for a Mathematics in Our Lives curriculum unit, in which students learn about ordered pairs in graphing by plotting points related to their lived experiences. The language objectives are to orally describe and write five sentences explaining five important events in their lives. The content objectives are to identify and label the x and y axes and graph ordered pairs represented in Quadrant I. The steps, as illustrated in Figures 8.1 and 8.2, include the following:

- Look at examples of life graphs other students have created.
- Model/think-aloud: What are some of the most important events that have happened in my life?
- Partner brainstorm: What are some of the most important events that have happened in your life?
- Write at least five ideas (phrases) on the chart. Fill in your age at the time.
- Discuss the word "rate." Direct the class to a website that introduces students to the concept of "rating" through an interactive game-like activity.
- Rate each life event by importance on a scale of zero to ten.
- Write ordered pairs for each life event, X axis = time; Y axis = rating.
- Explore your graph with partner and make observations.
- Label the graph.
- Model plotting points using ordered pairs on your graph.
- Plot ordered pairs on the graph.
- Create small illustrations to explain each ordered pair.
- Share life graphs with small group.

Reflect on the Mathematics in our Lives lesson:

a. In what ways is this project similar to and/or different from the three projects discussed in this chapter?

b. Fill out the MALP Checklist for this project. Refer to the completed checklists at the end of the chapter as resources.

Important events in my life	How old was I? (x)	Rate (y)
Teacher's Example: College graduation	21	8
Baby brother born	3	7
Come to america	11	9
Grandfather die	7	8
Start job in restaurant	14	6
Take english test	16	4

Figure 8.1. Mathematics in Our Lives—Life Events Chart

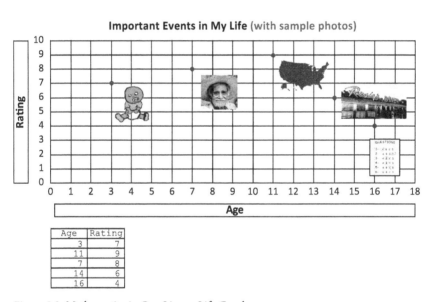

Figure 8.2. Mathematics in Our Lives—Life Graph

4. Dr. Jill Watson has developed the RISA Protocol, designed to leverage the orality of SLIFE to help them access academic language and content. RISA refers to Routine, Integrated, Structured, Academic interaction, whereby teachers make the protocol a part of their regular weekly routine, and integrate it with their content objectives, giving students a structured template for their interaction, and ensuring they use both academic vocabulary and academic structures. The steps for the RISA Protocol include the following:
   1. Hang a poster with the dialogue on it.
   2. Give students a paper copy of the dialogue.

3. Post key vocabulary related to unit and dialogue.
4. Explain the dialogue briefly.
5. Model correct, natural pronunciation and prosody of words and key phrases.
6. Have the class repeat the dialogue chorally while pointing to each word.
7. Model the format with one student, and then another.
8. Have two students perform the dialogue for the class. Have two more do the same dialogue for the class.
9. Assign partners.
10. Have all members of the class do the dialogue with their partner while you and classroom cultural liaisons circulate and support.
11. Always have students end with a handshake or air-shake!

Here is a sample RISA dialogue between two students, designated as A and B:

Map Skills Dialogue

A: Can you please help me study my map vocabulary?
B: I'd be happy to help.

A: Thanks, my friend! What are latitude lines?
B: Latitude lines are _____. Now you tell me the definition.

A: Latitude lines are _____. What are longitude lines?
B: Longitude lines are _____. Your turn.

A: Longitude lines are _____. What is the equator?
B: The equator is _____. Now you say it.

A: The equator is _____. What is the prime meridian?
B: The prime meridian is _____. Your turn!

A: The prime meridian is _____. What is a compass rose?
B: A compass rose is _____. Now you tell me.

A: A compass rose is _____. OK, that's all I have. Thanks for helping me!
B: My pleasure! I think you'll do great on your test!

Reflect on Dr. Watson's RISA Protocol
a. In what ways is RISA consistent with the MALP approach?
b. Consider how you might include RISA in a project.

9. Reflecting on MALP

We have elucidated a new instructional approach, MALP, and examined the balancing of language, content, and culture in addressing the needs of SLIFE in this book.

As they adapt to formal education, there are certain things SLIFE must learn—notably, to regard and use print as a primary resource for information and as a vehicle for communication, and to be individually accountable for their work. The best way to transition them is to incorporate their preferred ways of learning, oral transmission and shared responsibility, into our teaching and gradually accustom them to the ways of formal education. MALP transitions the students to print—not just by teaching and rehearsing the basics of print literacy, but by making strong connections between oral transmission and the written word. In addition, and perhaps most important for their ultimate success, because SLIFE are unfamiliar with decontextualized tasks and associated academic ways of thinking, teachers must provide them with extensive opportunities to learn and to practice via tasks that use familiar language and content. Doing so allows SLIFE to focus on the task itself and not become distracted by other unfamiliar elements. It is this third component of MALP that requires an understanding of the balancing of the three schemata: linguistic, content, and formal, so that teachers can plan activities to focus exclusively on the hidden challenge, namely new formal schemata.

Ms. Kempinski Makes the Journey

My New Favorite Class

Despite the realities facing them regarding curriculum, placement of students, and standardized testing requirements, teachers of SLIFE are choosing to implement MALP and are finding that the investment in adapting their teaching is worthwhile when they look at the results in terms of student motivation and accomplishment (Marshall, DeCapua & Antolini, 2010; Marshall & DeCapua, 2018). One such teacher is Ms. Kempinski who transformed her teaching after professional development training in MALP. When we first met Ms. Kempinski, she was faced with a high school math class of twenty beginner ELs, all of whom had been identified as SLIFE. Ms. Kempinski was mandated to teach this class of SLIFE integrated algebra, yet most of them were still struggling with basic operations.

In her other math classes, Ms. Kempinski taught with very positive results; however, in this particular class, she asked for assistance in the form of professional development. Her main concern was content and, to a lesser extent, language. In our initial meeting with her, she expressed her general frustrations:

> Some come late. If they are on time they don't bring a pencil, the majority don't do homework, and I can't get them to listen to me regarding their behavior. How can I help them be successful if the basics are not there?

Let us take a look at one of the early lessons we observed. We enter the classroom and see the chairs in rows and on the wall a commercially made poster encouraging students to do their homework. Students drift in slowly and wait at their desks until Ms. Kempinski reminds them to look at the math problems on the board and begin their work. This lesson, like all her lessons, begins with an activity called Do Now, followed by a presentation on the lesson topic for the day, practice problems, and finally, a homework assignment. This scripted approach is the one uniformly implemented in her large urban high school.

For the Do Now portion of the lesson, Ms. Kempinski begins with three problems from the previous lesson written on the board. The class has just started to discuss the rules for the order in which to solve mathematical problems, known as the Order of Operations principle. The students complete the problems on their own at their desks. When the allotted time is up, Ms. Kempinski reviews each problem by calling on an individual student to tell her the answer or write the answer on the board. She follows this activity with a lecture presentation on a new type of math problem they will learn that day. As she lectures, she demonstrates how to complete the new problems using examples that she writes on the board. The new problems still focus on the Order of Operations but are more difficult than the previous ones, as these involve additional, more complex operations. She instructs the students to copy what she writes on the board into their notebooks. After she has explained and demonstrated this new type of problem, Ms. Kempinski does three additional ones, calling on individual students to volunteer as the class goes through the problems together on the board, step-by-step. There is virtually no time for questions and answers as there barely is time to go through the problems, given that she must allot a specific amount of time each day for students to practice solving problems individually.

Once the class has completed the three additional problems on the board together, Ms. Kempinski hands out a worksheet and instructs the students that they have until the end of the period to practice similar problems on their own. While they are working alone on their worksheets, she circulates around the room to help those who raise their hands for help, reviewing again individually how to solve the problems. When students have completed their worksheets and Ms. Kempinski has checked their work, she selects students to go to the board to put up one of the practice problems for the rest of the class to see. Ms. Kempinski reminds the students to check the board to see if they solved the problems correctly and to copy anything they missed into their math notebooks to help them do the homework they will have for tomorrow's class. At the end of class, Ms. Kempinski hands out another worksheet with similar problems for the students to complete as their homework assignment.

Our first impression was that Ms. Kempinski was a very knowledgeable, organized teacher. Her lesson moved along efficiently, and she was intent on presenting the material as clearly as possible. It also struck us immediately that this was a very teacher-centered classroom, with minimal student input. Although she tried to help students individually as they struggled to complete the worksheet, Ms. Kempinski had not allowed for peer interaction and support, had not made direct connections between oral and written modes, and had not made explicit new academic ways of thinking—pedagogical considerations very important for SLIFE.

We now enter Ms. Kempinski's classroom several months later, after she has participated in MALP-based professional development training. Today, we immediately see a learning community. There is a monthly calendar hanging showing birthdays, holidays, and key assignment dates. The walls display completed student projects. There is a chart with sentence frames as a guide for the students. Before beginning the lesson, Ms. Kempinski has referred to her binder containing notes about each student, along with that student's math issues as they relate to the current work in the unit. She pairs the students based on what they can do for each other in terms of math, language, or both.

In this new unit, the class is going to be introduced to *like terms* and *unlike terms* to see what the criteria are for differentiating them. In mathematics, a *term* is any number (3), variable (x), or combination (3xy), with or without an exponent ($3x^2$). This concept relates to comparison and contrast, the key academic way of thinking on which Ms. Kempinski will focus. She asks students to practice by listing some ways that they, as individuals, are similar to or different from each other. After this, she points out that they can select the criteria they want to use—native language, native country, height, number of people in their family, and so on. She then points out that in math, by contrast, there are set criteria that must be used to decide if two mathematical terms are alike or not.

She is now ready to introduce the decontextualized math concept of like and unlike terms. Ms. Kempinski focuses on the word *term*. As she says each part of the term and points to it, she labels each part of a sample term: *coefficient, variable, exponent*. She calls attention to why it is important to know if two terms are alike by asking, "Can we add them together or 'combine' them?"

Ms. Kempinski also addresses the issue of what parts of the term matter, referring back to the concept of *set criteria* she had reviewed previously. Because, in previous lessons, Ms. Kempinski has carefully scaffolded the several parts of a mathematical term, that is, the coefficient, the variable, and the exponent, and provided sentence frames for them to use in responding to the examples, the students are able to focus on the new concept—like and unlike terms.

Each pair of students produces a poster for the unit, using a template Ms. Kempinski has supplied. The students provide their own examples of like and unlike terms. She gives each pair terms to analyze and the criteria they are to use to determine the placement of a term in that category. On their posters, they must include their responses to three items: (a) are they like terms? (b) tell how you know; and (c) combine or rewrite the expression. For item (b), they need be able to state the criteria they used to decide if the terms were like or unlike; that is, whether they have the same variable and the same exponent or not. The groups present their posters to each other, which then go up on the wall for reference. In this lesson on like and unlike terms, students were able to manage the new concept of combining only like terms because Ms. Kempinski had focused earlier on basic and essential mathematical terminology—coefficient, variable, exponent. While most of her fellow math teachers assumed that students would be familiar with this vocabulary by the time they were in high school, she did not assume any prior knowledge and ensured she introduced everything, knowing that almost everything was a totally new concept for SLIFE.

Ms. Kempinski has incorporated the main points from this book into her teaching. She uses the three components of MALP: Accept the Conditions; Combine the Processes; and Target New Activities for Learning. Her classroom is now one that focuses on projects. Reflecting on her most challenging class, Ms. Kempinski tells us:

This is my new favorite class—we really have a good time and they actually get it! It makes such as difference to teach this way. For SLIFE who were failing, I can see real progress; they still take longer than other ELs to catch on, but they are trying and succeeding over time. I now have a 60 percent pass rate in that class, up from only 20 percent before.

In working with teachers of SLIFE on lessons and projects, such as those presented in this text, we have found multiple benefits from using the MALP Teacher Planning Checklist. As they carefully review the MALP instructional approach, teachers identify specific aspects of their teaching that incorporate each of the elements. This, in turn, ensures that they are infusing all the elements of MALP into their lessons. The lesson and project analysis they conduct with the MALP Teacher Planning Checklist reinforces their understanding that the elements, when implemented together, result in promoting a positive learning experience for SLIFE. Ms. Kempinski's consistent use of the MALP Teacher Planning Checklist in preparing her lessons helped her ensure that she indeed incorporated the three components and six elements regularly, reducing the cultural dissonance of the students and better preparing them for learning.

Revisiting Cultural Dissonance

Chapter 1 presented a chart of what teachers and learners in most formal classrooms assume about the goals of K–12 instruction and what learners bring to the classroom. In this book, we have explored each of these assumptions, how they differ for SLIFE, and how teachers can transition them to their new educational setting.

As we have emphasized, MALP is an instructional approach that calls for adaptation on the part of both the teachers and their students to reduce cultural dissonance. Although we have focused largely on how the teacher must adjust and adapt as an instructor to implement MALP, it is, of course, also vital for SLIFE to adjust and adapt. They must transition to feeling comfortable with, and becoming accustomed to, print as a primary resource, individual accountability, and decontextualized tasks and associated academic ways of thinking.

Figure 9.1, Ways of Learning Continuum, shows two divergent perspectives on SLIFE with respect to their experiences in formal education. The right end of the continuum represents the formal educational learning paradigm. The left end represents the informal learning paradigm of SLIFE. The center of the continuum illustrates where SLIFE are in schools today. The deficit perspective is illustrated by arrow #1 pointing back to the left. In this view, SLIFE are seen as sharing the assumptions about education and the learning paradigm of the formal educational system but failing to achieve success. However, SLIFE do not approach education from the right end, which is unfamiliar to them. Rather, most SLIFE begin at the left end of the continuum, where, as members of collectivistic cultures who have little or no formal education, they have to move toward the other end, toward an individualistic culture and

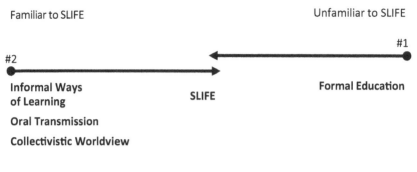

(Adapted from Marshall & DeCapua, 2013)

Figure 9.1. Ways of Learning Continuum

academic ways of thinking, when they find themselves in formal classrooms. This perspective is illustrated by arrow #2, showing SLIFE as bringing their familiar learning paradigm with them as they move along the continuum of ways of learning. Far from being deficient learners, these students have simply been accustomed to a very different way of learning. They have actually made credible attempts to move along the continuum to the right despite the challenges they face.

The continuum emphasizes that SLIFE have their own set of assumptions about teaching and learning. Yet, neither SLIFE nor their teachers necessarily realize that (a) they have these assumptions; and that (b) the assumptions each group has are very different. MALP makes these different assumptions explicit, views teaching and learning on a cultural continuum, and offers a mutually adaptive approach that meets SLIFE halfway and helps transition them to the right side of the continuum. For these students, MALP offers a pathway to success. It is essential that educators see SLIFE as students who are coming from a different end of the continuum with a very different paradigm and who are moving *toward* the learning paradigm of formal education. SLIFE, in addition to academic issues, are confronting cultural issues of learning. (We encourage readers to refer DeCapua, Marshall & Tang (2020) for more extensive discussion and examples of SLIFE on the Ways of Learning Continuum. We also suggest that those involved in teacher preparation refer to DeCapua & Marshall (2022) for a discussion of how to promote awareness and understanding of SLIFE and the MALP instructional approach into their courses.)

We now look at Vuong, a student who has, like Ms. Kempinski, made a journey. In this case, the journey took him along the Ways of Learning Continuum toward the paradigm of formal education and academic success.

Vuong Makes the Journey

Education Is Just the Beginning ...

We first met Vuong in Chapter 1 when we read the first lines of his journal excerpt describing his initial experiences with print (see page 22). The son of a fisherman in Vietnam, Vuong came to this country as a teenager. Although he had had little formal schooling, he was placed into high school based on his age. Through his participation in content-area classes infused with MALP, he became successful over time, and eventually completed a two-year degree in automotive technology.

We close with Vuong's voice, beginning with the complete version of his journal excerpt, the first and last paragraph of which we saw in Chapter 1:

> The most importants I have learned about the United States that is a book, newspapers, or notebook and pens. These things are always let me know how to live here.

> I can remember once upon a time, that the first time I came here and I didn't know anything about the United States. At that time, I just pick up the textbooks from my teacher, and then I read it, but I didn't understand it much because I didn't study English before, at that times I picked up a dictionary to look up the words I didn't understand and translate by my native language ...

> ... I always remember the books are the most important things for me to learn when I live in the United States.

It is important to note that had Vuong been left to decipher the U.S. educational system on his own, he may have appeared to be learning but may not have truly shifted his paradigm. He benefited, however, from instructors trained in MALP who helped him move along the continuum of ways of learning.

Here is a page from Vuong's ESL journal, two years later, after extensive instruction in sheltered courses using MALP. Vuong produced this piece, again reflecting on his learning in the United States. MALP allowed him to gain insight into his new language, his new culture, and, in particular, his new future. He gave it the heading *Poemtry.*

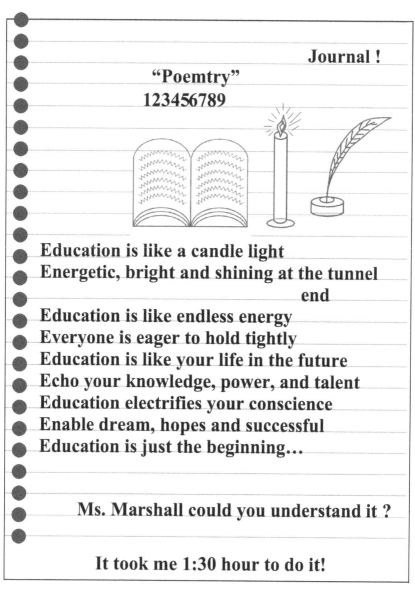

Journal !

"Poemtry"
123456789

Education is like a candle light
Energetic, bright and shining at the tunnel
end
Education is like endless energy
Everyone is eager to hold tightly
Education is like your life in the future
Echo your knowledge, power, and talent
Education electrifies your conscience
Enable dream, hopes and successful
Education is just the beginning…

Ms. Marshall could you understand it ?

It took me 1:30 hour to do it!

Figure 9.2. Poemtry

For Further Exploration

1. As for any major shift in pedagogical orientation, sustained efforts must be made and supported, and positive results demonstrated, in order for innovations to take hold. Ms. Kempinski's supervisor provided administrative support, allowing her to restructure her lesson plans, have alternative seating arrangements, and take more time to build concepts.

   a. What issues and/or obstacles do you believe might prevent teachers from implementing MALP in your school?

   b. How could you address these issues and gain support for the MALP instructional approach? Reflect on what you have learned from this text as support.

2. While we began to develop this approach as we sat in classrooms watching and listening—seeing SLIFE as disengaged learners, their potential not realized—we have come to believe that the approach has possibilities for other learners as well. If we return to our notion of a continuum of ways of learning presented in this chapter, we can imagine that there are other students who are perhaps not as obviously experiencing cultural dissonance, but who also find themselves uncomfortable with the classroom setting. Think of other students you know who are not SLIFE but who are also struggling learners.

   a. Where would you place them on the continuum? Explain.

   b. Do you think they could benefit from the MALP instructional approach? Why or why not?

3. Teachers often tell us that they have SLIFE who are not ELs but speakers of English dialects, or Creoles such as Jamaicans, Liberians, or Guyanese. They wonder whether these students, too, might benefit from MALP. Consider what you have learned in this book.

   a. How could MALP help English-speaking SLIFE? Be specific and provide examples.

   b. What adjustments would you make if you were using MALP for this population?

   c. Using a lesson you have taught or have seen taught, explain how you would incorporate MALP for these SLIFE.

4. The overrepresentation and/or underrepresentation of ELs in special education has been a concern for some time (see e.g., Sanatullova-Allison & Robison-Young, 2016). These concerns are even more applicable to SLIFE since they are difficult to diagnose because of additional factors that may come into play, such as reading and writing skills and/or subject area knowledge.

   a. In your experience, what are some of the issues in trying to determine if a SLIFE might need special education? Interview other English language teachers and guidance counselors to get their perspectives on referrals of ELs and SLIFE to special education.

   b. If you have a class of SLIFE that includes students dually identified as special education students as well as SLIFE, take notes on how they respond as you implement MALP in your classroom.

   c. Identify aspects of MALP that may assist in shedding light on the misclassification of SLIFE as in need of special education services.

5. Reread the poem by Vuong. Reconsider his journal entry from two years earlier.

   a. How do these two writing samples reflect the paradigm shift for this student? Cite examples from the text to illustrate specific ways in which the student has embraced the learning paradigm of formal education. Notice not only language and content, which are themselves quite relevant, but also the type of thinking Vuong is doing as he composes his piece.

   b. Consider the note that Vuong wrote below his poem.

> Teacher, could you understand it?
> It took me 1:30 to do it!

Revisit his two pieces of writing, and think about why he included the note, what he was trying to convey by it, and how it further illustrates that he has made the journey to formal education successfully.

Appendix A: MALP® Teacher Planning Checklist

MALP Teacher Planning Checklist
Mutually Adaptive Learning Paradigm®

A. Accept Conditions for Learning
A1. I am making this lesson/project immediately relevant to my students' lives. Explain:
A2. I am helping students develop and maintain interconnectedness with each other. Explain:

B. Combine Processes for Learning
B1. I am incorporating both shared responsibility and individual accountability. Explain:
B2. I am scaffolding the written word through oral interaction. Explain:

C. Target New Activities for Learning
C1. I am teaching students to develop academic ways of thinking. Explain:
C2. I am teaching students to engage in decontextualized tasks to demonstrate mastery. Explain:
C3. I am using familiar language and content as scaffolds. Explain:

Revised from © DeCapua, A. & Marshall, H.W. (2011). *Breaking New Ground: Teaching Students with Limited or Interrupted Formal Education in Secondary Schools,* University of Michigan Press, (p.68). For terms and conditions of use, contact information@malpeducation.com

References

Abi-Hashem, N. (2018). Trauma, coping, and resiliency among Syrian refugees in Lebanon and beyond: A profile of the Syrian nation at war. Rich, G. J. & Sirikantraporn, S. J. (eds.). *Human Strengths and Resilience: Developmental, Cross-Cultural, and International Perspectives.* Lexington Books/Rowman & Littlefield, (pp. 105–130).

Alderson, J. C. (2000). *Assessing Reading.* Cambridge University Press.

Altherr Flores, J. (2017). Social semiotics and multimodal assessment of L2 adult emergent readers from refugee backgrounds. Sosiński, M. (hrsg.), *Alfabetación y aprendizaje de idiomas por adultos: Investigación, política educativa y práctica docente.* Granada: Proceedings of the 2016 LESLLA Symposium, (S. pp. 9–31). https://drive.google.com/drive/folders/13TKI9 9J6Urlq73IvmQTKz50QLxjEEM9t

Anderson, N. J. (1999). *Exploring Second Language Reading.* Heinle & Heinle.

Anderson-Levitt, K. (2003). A world culture of schooling? *Local Meanings, Global Schooling: Anthropology and World Culture Theory.* Palgrave Macmillan, (pp. 1–26). https://doi.org/10.1057/9781403980359_1

Anderson, L. W. (ed.), Krathwohl, D. R. (ed.), Airasian, P., Cruikshank, K., Mayer, R., Pintrich, P., Raths, J. & Wittrock, M. (2001). *A Taxonomy for Learning, Teaching, and Assessing: A Revision of Bloom's Taxonomy of Educational Objectives* (Complete Edition). Longman.

Andrews, M. (2016). Three cultural models of teacher interaction valued by Mexican students at a US high school. *Race Ethnicity and Education. 19*(2), (pp. 368–388). https://DOI.org/10.1080/13613324.2013.843519

Arevalo, E., So, D. & McNaughton-Cassill, M. (2016). The role of collectivism among Latino American college students. *Journal of Latinos and Education. 15*(1), (pp. 3–11). https://DOI.org/10.1080/15348431.2015.1045143

Baker, D. & LeTendre, G. K. (2005). *National Differences, Global Similarities: World Culture and the Future of Schooling.* Stanford University Press.

Bigelow, M. & Vinogradov, P. (2011). Teaching adult second language learners who are emergent readers. *Annual Review of Applied Linguistics. 31*, (pp. 120–136). https://DOI.org/10.1017/S0267190511000109

Birman, D. & Tran, N. (2017). When worlds collide: Academic adjustment of Somalia Bantu students with limited formal education in a U.S. elementary school. *International Journal of Intercultural Relations.* 60, (pp. 132–144). http://dx.DOI.org/10.1016/j.ijintrel.2017.06.008

Bloom, B. (1956). *Taxonomy of Educational Objectives, Handbook I: The Cognitive Domain.* David McKay.

Bower, V. (ed.). (2014). *Developing Early Literacy 0–8: From Theory to Practice.* Sage.

Brewer, C. A. & McCabe, M. (2014). *Immigrant and Refugee Students in Canada.* Brush Education.

Browder, C. (2019). The trouble with operationalizing people: My research with students with limited or interrupted formal education (SLIFE). Warriner, D. & Bigelow, M. (eds.). *Critical Reflections on Research Methods: Power and Equity in Complex Multilingual Contexts.* Multilingual Matters, (pp. 43–52).

Browder, C., Pentón Herrera, L. J. & Franco, J. (2022). Advancing the conversation: Humanizing and problematizing the conversation about the students we call SLIFE. Pentón Herrera, L. J. (ed.). *English and Students with Limited or Interrupted Formal Education: Global Perspectives on Teacher Preparation and Classroom Practices.* Springer, (pp. 9–17).

Broussard, P. (Nov. 12, 2020). SLIFE: More than one lens. Seidlitz Education Virtual SLIFE Conference.

Cavallaro, C. & Sembiante, S. (2020). Facilitating culturally sustaining, functional literacy practices in a middle school ESOL reading program: A design-based research study. *Language and Education.* 35(3), (pp. 1–20). https://DOI.org/10.1080/09500782.2020.1775244

Cazden, C. (2001). *Classroom Discourse: The Language of Teaching and Learning* (2nd ed.). Heinemann.

Cenoz, J. (2015). Content-based instruction and content and language integrated learning: The same or different? *Language, Culture and Curriculum.* 28(1), (pp. 8–24). https://DOI.org/10.1080/07908318.2014.1000922

Chavajay, P. & Rogoff, B. (2002). Schooling and traditional collaborative social organization of problem solving by Mayan mothers and children. *Developmental Psychology.* 38(1), (pp. 55–66). https://DOI.org/10.1037/0012-1649.38.1.55

Clarke, M. (2007). *Common Ground, Contested Territory: Examining Roles of English Language Teachers in Troubled Times.* University of Michigan Press.

Cole, M. (2005). Cross-cultural and historical perspectives on the developmental consequences of education. *Human Development.* 48(4), (pp. 195–216). https://DOI.org/10.1159/000086855

Crandall, B. (2018). "History should come first": Perspectives of Somali-born, refugee-background male youth on writing in and out of school. S. Shapiro,

R. Farrelly & M.J. Curry (eds.). *Educating Refugee-background Students' Critical Issues and Dynamic Contexts*. Multilingual Matters, (pp. 33–48).

Croce, K. A. (2018). Refugee students arrive at a school: What happens next? *Global Education Review*. 5(4), (pp. 7–16).

Dávila, L. (2012). For them it's sink or swim: Refugee students and the dynamics of migration, and (dis)placement in school. *Power and Education*. 4(2), (pp. 139–149). http://DOI.org/10.2304/power.2012.4.2.139

DeCapua, A. (2019). *SLIFE: What Every Teacher Needs to Know*. E-book. University of Michigan Press.

DeCapua, A. (2018). *Culture Myths: Applying Second Language Research to Classroom Teaching*. University of Michigan Press.

DeCapua, A. (2017). *Grammar for Teachers: A guide to American English for Native and Non-native Speakers* (2nd ed.). Springer.

DeCapua, A. (2021). Students with limited or interrupted education (SLIFE). J. Govoni & C. Lovell (eds.). *Preparing the Way: Teaching ELs in the PreK-12 Classroom*. Kendall Hunt, (Chapter 3, pp. 91–117).

DeCapua, A. (2022). Students with limited or interrupted education (SLIFE). L. Shaqareq & T. Kimball (eds.). *Rooted in TESOL: Language, Culture, and Theories*. (Chapter 9). Kendall Hunt.

DeCapua, A. & Marshall, H. W. (2022). Making space for students with limited or interrupted formal education in teacher education. L. Pentón Herrera (ed.). *English and Students with Limited or Interrupted Formal Education: Global Perspectives on Teacher Preparation and Classroom Practices*. Springer, (pp. 125–139).

DeCapua, A. & Marshall, H. W. (2020). To define is to know. N. Pettit, R. Farrelly & A. Elson (eds.). *Literacy Education and Second Language Learning for Adults (LESLLA): Proceedings of the 15th Symposium*. Literacy education and second language learning for adults (LESLLA), (pp. 1–18). https://drive.google.com/drive/folders/1iST4hHYTrrB5yWFw8kSwJ0NBOFpsarcL

DeCapua, A. & Marshall, H. W. (2015). Reframing the conversation about students with limited or interrupted formal education: From achievement gap to cultural dissonance. *NASSP Bulletin*. 99(4), (pp. 356–370).

DeCapua, A. & Marshall, H. W. (2011). *Breaking New Ground: Students with Limited or Interrupted Formal Education in U.S. Secondary Schools* (1st ed.). University of Michigan Press.

DeCapua, A. & Marshall H. W. (2010). Serving ELLs with limited or interrupted education: Intervention that works. *TESOL Journal*. 1, (pp. 49–70).

DeCapua A. & McDonell T. (2008). There is more to an iceberg than the tip: Culture and second language writing in the classroom. J. Paull (ed.). *From Hip Hop to Hyperlinks: Practical Approaches for Teaching Culture in the Composition Classroom*. Cambridge Scholars Publications, (pp. 136–148).

DeCapua, A. & Triulzi, M. (2020). Learning for work: Hidden challenges for LESLLA learners. M. D'Agostino & E. Mocciaro (eds.). *Literacy Education and Second Language Learning for Adults (LESLLA): Proceedings of the 14th Symposium.* Digital Frontiers, (pp. 169–188).

DeCapua, A., Marshall, H. W. & Tang, F. L. (2020). *Meeting the Needs of SLIFE: A Guide for Educators* (2nd ed.). University of Michigan Press.

DeCapua, A., Smathers, W. & Tang, F. (2009). *Meeting the Needs of Students with Limited or Interrupted Schooling: A Guide for Educators* (1st ed.). University of Michigan Press.

DeCapua, A. & Wintergerst, A. (2016). *Crossing Cultures in the Language Classroom.* University of Michigan Press.

Denny, J. P. (1991). Rational thought in oral culture and literate decontextualization. D. Olson & N. Torrance (eds.). *Literacy and Orality.* Cambridge, (pp. 66–89).

de Souza, M. (2013). A case study of schooling practices at an escuela secundaria in Mexico. *The High School Journal. 96*(4), (pp. 302–320). https://DOI.org/10.1353/hsj.2013.0017

DeNicolo, C., Yu, M., Crowley C. & Gabel S. (2017). Reimagining critical care and problematizing sense of school belonging as a response to inequality for immigrants and children of immigrants. *Review of Research in Education. 41*(1), (pp. 500–530). DOI:10.3102/0091732X17690498

Durand, T. (2011). Latina mothers' cultural beliefs about their children, parental roles, and education: Implications for effective and empowering home-school partnerships. *Urban Review. 43*(2), (pp. 255–278). DOI.org/10.1007/s11256-010-0167-5

Echevarria, J., Vogt, M.E. & Short, D. (2016). *Making Content Comprehensible for English Learners: The SIOP Model.* Pearson.

Fagundes, F. (2007). Charles Reis Felix's "!rough a Portagee Gate"; Lives parceled out in stories. *MELUS. 32*(2), (pp. 151–163).

Ferguson-Patrick, K. (2020). Cooperative learning in Swedish classrooms: Engagement and relationships as a focus for culturally diverse students. *Education Sciences. 10*(11), (pp. 1–21). https://DOI.org/10.3390/educsci10110312

Farid, M. & McMahan, D. (2004). *Accommodating and Educating Somali Students in Minnesota: A Handbook for Teachers and Administrators.* Hamline University Press.

Flaitz, J. (2018). *Refugee Students: What Every Teacher Needs to Know.* University of Michigan Press.

Floyd, A. & Sakellariou, D. (2017). Healthcare access for refugee women with limited literacy: Layers of disadvantage. *International Journal for Equity in Health. 16*(1). https://DOI.org/10.1186/s12939-017-0694-8

Flynn, J. (2007). *What is Intelligence?* Cambridge University Press.

Frankel, K., Becker, B., Rowe M. & Pearson P. (2017). From "what is reading?" to what is literacy? *Journal of Education. 196*(3), (pp. 7–17). DOI:10.1177/0022057419600303

Freire, P. (2014). *Pedagogy of Hope: Reliving Pedagogy of the Oppressed.* Bloomsbury.

Fruja Amthor, R. & Roxas, K. (2016). Multicultural education and newcomer youth: Re-imagining a more inclusive vision for immigrant and refugee students. *Educational Studies. 52*(2), (pp. 155–176). https://DOI.org/10.1080/00131946.2016.1142992

Gagné, A., Al-Hashimi, N., Little, M., Lowen, M. & Sidhu, A. (2018). Educator perspectives on the social and academic integration of Syrian refugees in Canada. *Journal of Family Diversity in Education. 3*(1), (pp. 48–76). https://doi.org/10.53956/jfde.2018.124

Gahungu, A., Gahungu, O. & Luseno, F. (2011). Educating culturally displaced students with truncated formal education (CDS-TFE): The case of refugee students and challenges for administrators, teachers, and counselors. *International Journal of Educational Leadership Preparation. 6*(2), (pp. 1–19). https://files.eric.ed.gov/fulltext/EJ973832.pdf

Gándara, P. (2020). The students we share: Falling through the cracks on both sides of the US-Mexico border. *Ethnic and Racial Studies. 43*(1), 3859. DOI:10.1080/01419870.2019.1667514

Garcia, O. & Wei, L. (2014). *Translanguaging: Language, Bilingualism and Education.* Palgrave Macmillan.

Gay, G. (2018). *Culturally Responsive Teaching: Theory, Research and Practice* (3rd ed.). Teachers College Press.

Gay, G. (2000). *Culturally Responsive Teaching: Theory, Research and Practice.* Teachers College Press.

Gillies, R. M. (2016). Cooperative learning: Review of research and practice. *Australian Journal of Teacher Education. 41*(3). http://dx.DOI.org/10.14221/ajte.2016v41n3.3

Gonzales, S. & Shields, C. (2015). Education "reform" in Latino Detroit: Achievement gap or colonial legacy? *Race, Ethnicity and Education. 18*(3), (pp. 21–340). DOI: 10.1080/13613324.2014.911170

González, R. & Ayala- Alcantar, C. (2008). Critical caring: Dispelling Latino stereotypes among preservice teachers. *Journal of Latinos and Education. 7*(2), (pp. 129–143). DOI:10.1080/ 15348430701828699

González, N., Moll, L. & Amanti, C. (2005). *Funds of Knowledge: Theorizing Practices in Households, Communities, and Classrooms.* Lawrence Erlbaum.

Greenfield, P. M. & Quiroz, B. (2013). Context and culture in the socialization and development of personal achievement values: Comparing Latino immigrant families, European American families, and elementary school teachers. *Journal of Applied Developmental Psychology. 34*(2), (pp. 108–118). https://DOI.org/10.1016/j.appdev.2012.11.002

Gu, Q. (2010). Variations in beliefs and practices: Teaching English in cross-cultural contexts. *Language and Intercultural Communication. 10*(1), (pp. 32–53). https://DOI.org/10.1080/14708470903377357

Hall, E. (1976). *Beyond Culture.* Anchor.

Hammond, A. (2014). *Culturally Responsive Teaching and the Brain: Promoting Authentic Engagement and Rigor Among Culturally and Linguistically Diverse Students.* Corwin.

Hanewald, R. (2013). Transition between primary and secondary school: Why it is important and how it can be supported? *Australian Journal of Teacher Education. 38*(1). http://dx.DOI.org/10.14221/ajte.2013v38n1.7

Harklau, L. (2016). Bureaucratic dysfunctions in the education of Latino immigrant youth. *American Journal of Education. 122*(4), (pp. 601–627). https://www.jstor.org/stable/26544511

Hoffman, M. (2019). Including multiple literacies in the classroom. *European Journal of Applied Linguistics and TEFL. 8*(1), (pp. 21–37).

Hofstede, G. (2001). *Culture's Consequences: Comparing Values, Behaviors, Institutions, and Organizations Across Nations.* Sage.

Hos, R. (2020). The lives, aspirations, and needs of refugee and immigrant students with interrupted formal education (SLIFE) in a secondary newcomer program. *Urban Education. 55*(7), (pp. 1021–1044). https://DOI.org/10.1177/0042085916666932

Huang, G. H. C. & Lam, E. T. C. (2022). Resettled refugee families: Parenting practices and educational involvement. *10*(6), (pp. 181–195). DOI:10.4236/jss.2022.106015

Hughes, M. & Greenhough, P. (2006). Boxes, bags and videotape: Enhancing home-school communication through knowledge exchange activities. *Educational Review. 58,* (pp. 471–487). https://doi.org/10.1080/00131910600971958

Huma, A. (2016). Cultural scripts resist reforms in teacher education. *Journal of Education and Practice. 7*(18), (pp. 26–31). https://core.ac.uk/download/pdf/234639049.pdf

Ibarra, R. (2001). *Beyond Affirmative Action: Reframing the Context of Higher Education.* University of Wisconsin Press.

Jacobs, G. M. & Renandya, W. (2019). *Student Centered Cooperative Learning: Linking Concepts in Education to Promote Student Learning.* Springer.

James, M. O. (1987). ESL reading pedagogy: Implications of schema-theoretical research. J. Devine, P. Carrell & D. Eskey (eds.). *Research in Reading in English as a Second Language.* TESOL, (pp. 175–188).

Jiménez-Balam, D., Alcalá, L. & Salgado, D. (2019). Maya children's medicinal plant knowledge: Initiative and agency in their learning process. *Learning, Culture, and Social Interaction. 22*, 100333. https://DOI.org/10.1016/j.lcsi.2019.100333

Johnson, D. & Johnson, F. (2017). *Joining Together: Group Theory and Group Skills* (12th ed.). Pearson.

Kaiper-Marquez, A. (2020). Education and literacy as metonyms for English: Adult basic education and domestic workers in South Africa. Pettit, N., Farrelly, R. & Elson, A. (eds.). *Literacy Education and Second Language Learning for Adults (LESLLA): Proceedings of the Fifteenth Symposium.* LESLLA, (pp. 108–125).

Keengwe, J. & Onchwari, G. (2017). *Handbook of Research on Learner- Centered Pedagogy in Teacher Education and Professional Development.* IGA Global.

Kibler, K. W., (2019). *Teachers' experiences in serving late-entering Central American refugees with limited or interrupted formal education.* ProQuest Dissertations and Theses. https://scholarship.miami.edu/esploro/outputs/doctoral/Teachers-Experiences-in-Serving-Late-Entering-Central/991031447257602976

Koch, J. (2007). How schools can best support Somali students and their families. *International Journal of Multicultural Education. 9*(1), (pp. 1–15). https://DOI.org/10.18251/ijme.v9i1.8

Koehler, C. & Schneider, J. (2019). Young refugees in education: The particular challenges of school systems in Europe. *Comparative Migration Studies. 7*(28), (p. 28). https://comparativemigrationstudies.springeropen.com/track/pdf/10.1186/s40878-019-0129-3.pdf

Krahenbuhl, K. (2016). Student-centered education and constructivism: Challenges, concerns, and clarity for teachers. *The Clearing House: A Journal of Educational Strategies, Issues and Ideas. 89*(3), (pp. 97–105). DOI: 10.1080/00098655.2016.1191311

Kumaravadivelu, B. (2011). *Global Society: A Modular Model for Knowing, Analyzing, Recognizing, Doing, and Seeing.* Taylor & Francis.

Ladson-Billings, G. (1995). Toward a theory of culturally relevant pedagogy. *American Educational Research Journal. 32*, (pp. 465–491). https://DOI.org/10.3102/00028312032003465

Lakoff, G. (1987). *Women, Fire, and Other Dangerous Things.* University of Chicago.

Ledger, S. & Montero, M. K. (2022). Transforming ESL pedagogies: A teacher's journey from subject-centered to student-centered pedagogy when teaching print literacy to SLIFE. In Pentón Herrera, L. (ed.). *English and Students with Limited or Interrupted Formal Education: Global Perspectives on Teacher Preparation and Classroom Practices.* Springer, (pp. 141–159).

Lee, C.D., Meltzoff & Kuhl, P. (2022). The braid of human development: Neurophysiological processes and participation in cultural practices. Nasir, N. S., Lee, C. D., Pea, R. & McKinney de Royston, M. (eds.). (2020). *Handbook of the Cultural Foundations of Learning.* Routledge, (pp. 24–43).

Legare, C. & Harris, P. (2016). The ontogeny of cultural learning. *Child Development. 87*(3), (pp. 633–642). DOI: 10.1111/cdev.12542

Levi, T. K. (2019). Preparing pre-service teachers to support children with refugee experiences. *Alberta Journal of Educational Research. 65*(4), (pp. 285–304). doi.org/10.11575/ajer.v65i4.56554

Li, J. (2012). *Cultural Foundations of Learning: East and West.* Cambridge.

Li, X. & Grineva, M. (2017). Academic and social adjustment of high school refugee youth in Newfoundland. *TESL Canada Journal. 34*(1), (pp. 51–71). https://doi.org/10.18806/tesl.v34i1.1255

Linville, H. & Pentón Herrera, L. J. (2022). Why, how and where to advocate for English learners with limited or interrupted formal education. Pentón Herrera, L. J. (ed.). *English and Students with Limited or Interrupted Formal Education: Global Perspectives on Teacher Preparation and Classroom Practices.* Springer, (pp. 61–82).

Loughran, J. (2017). Quality in teacher education: Challenging assumptions, building understanding through foundation principles. Zhu, L., Goodwin, A. L. & Zhong, H. (eds.). *Quality of Teacher Education and Learning: Theory and Practice.* Springer, (pp. 69–84).

Loy, L. N. K. & Ye, J. (2017). The historical context of the role and status of scholars and teachers in traditional China. Zhu, L., Goodwin, A. L. & Zhong, H. (eds.). *Quality of Teacher Education and Learning: Theory and Practice.* Springer, (pp. 157–192).

Lujan, J. (2008). Linguistic and cultural adaptation needs of Mexican American students related to multiple-choice tests. *Journal of Nursing Education. 47*, (pp. 327–330). https://doi.org/10.3928/01484834-20080701-07

Lukes, M. (2021). Deconstructing the dropout factory: Redesigning secondary schools to better serve immigrant youth: Examples from the US context. Heidrich, L., Karakaşoğlu, Y., Mecheril, P. & Shure, S. (eds.). *Regimes of Belonging – Schools – Migrations.* Springer. https://doi.org/10.1007/978-3-658-29189-1_16

Luria, A. R. (1979). *The Making of Mind.* Harvard University Press.

Luster, T., Saltarelli, A., Rana, M., Qin, D., Bates, L. & Burdick, K. (2009). The experiences of Sudanese unaccompanied minors in foster care. *Journal of Family Psychology. 23*(3), (pp. 386–395). https://doi.org/10.1037/a0015570

Madziva, R. & Thondhlana, J. (2017). Provision of quality education in the context of Syrian refugee children in the UK: Opportunities and challenges. *Compare. 47*(6), (pp. 942–961). https://doi.org/10.1080/03057925.2017.1375848

Makarova, E. & Herzog, W. (2013). Hidden school dropout among immigrant students: A cross-sectional study. *Intercultural Education.* 24(6), (pp. 559–572). https://doi.org/10.1080/14675986.2013.867603

Marinellie, S. A. (2010). The understanding of word definitions in school age children. *Journal of Psycholinguistic Research.* 39(3), (pp. 179–97). http://dx.doi.org/10.1007/s10936-009-9132-4

Marshall, H. W. (1998). A mutually adaptive learning paradigm (MALP) for Hmong students. *Cultural Circles.* 3, (pp. 134–149). https://files.eric.ed.gov/fulltext/ED505352.pdf

Marshall, H. W. & DeCapua, A. (2018). Promoting achievement for struggling ESL students: Five recommendations. http://newsmanager.commpartners.com/tesolssis/issues/2018-04-24/1.html

Marshall, H. W. & DeCapua, A. (2013). *Making the Transition to Classroom Success: Culturally Responsive Teaching for Struggling Language Learners.* University of Michigan Press.

Marshall, H. W. & DeCapua, A. (2010). The newcomer booklet: A project for limited formally schooled students. *ELT Journal.* 64(4), (pp. 396–404). https://doi.org/10.1093/elt/ccp100

Marshall, H. W., DeCapua, A. & Antolini, C. (2010). Engaging English language learners with limited or interrupted formal education. *Educator's Voice.* 3, (pp. 56–65). https://www.nysut.org/~/media/files/nysut/resources/2010/may/educators-voice-3-adolescents/educatorsvoice3_adolescents_08_ell2.pdf?la=en

Martinez, I. (2016). Supporting two households: Unaccompanied Mexican minors and their absences from U.S. schools. *Journal of Latinos and Education.* 15(3), (pp. 229–243). http://dx.doi.org/10.1080/15348431.2015.1131690

Martinello, M. (2008). Language and the performance of English-language learners in math word problems. *Harvard Educational Review* 78(2), (pp. 333–368). https://doi.org/10.17763/haer.78.2.70783570r1111t32

Mejía-Arauz, R., Roberts, A. D. & Rogoff, B. (2012). Cultural variation in balance of nonverbal conversation and talk. *International Perspectives in Psychology: Research, Practice, Consultation.* 1(4), (pp. 207–220). https://doi.org/10.1037/a0030961

Mejía-Arauz, R., Rogoff, B., Dayton, A. & Henne-Ochoa, R. (2018). Collaboration or negotiation: two ways of interacting suggest how shared thinking develops. *Current Opinion in Psychology.* 23(1), (pp. 117–123). https://doi.org/10.1016/j.copsyc.2018.02.017

Menken, K. (2010). *English Learners Left Behind: Standardized Testing as Language Policy.* Multilingual Matters.

Meyer, B., Haywood, N., Sachdev, D. & Faraday, S. (2008). *Independent Learning: Literature Review.* Department for Children, Schools and

Families. Research Report DCSF-RR051. https://www.associationforpsy chologyteachers.com/uploads/4/5/6/6/4566919/independence_learning_ lit_review.pdf

Moll, L., Amanti, C., Neff, D. & Gonzalez, N. (1992). Funds of knowledge for teaching: Using a qualitative approach to connect homes and classrooms. *Theory into Practice. 31*, (pp. 132–141). https://doi.org/10.1080/004058 49209543534

Moll, L. & Greenberg, J. (1990). Creating zones of possibilities: Combining social contexts for instruction. Moll, L. (ed.). *Vygotsky and Education.* Cambridge, (pp. 319–348).

Montero, K., Newmaster, S. & Ledger, S. (2014). Exploring early reading instructional strategies to advance the print literacy development of adolescent SLIFE. *Journal of Adolescent & Adult Literacy. 58*, (pp. 59–69). https://doi.org/10.1002/jaal.318

Motti-Stefanidi, F. & Masten, A. S. (2013). School success and school engagement of immigrant children and adolescents: A risk and resilience developmental perspective. *European Psychologist. 18*(2), (pp. 126–135). https://doi.org/10.1027/1016-9040/a000139

Nag, S., Vagh, S. B., Dulay, K. & Snowling, M. (2019). Home language, school language and children's literacy attainments: A systematic review of evidence from low- and middle-income countries. *Review of Education. 7*, (pp. 91–150). https://doi.org/10.1002/rev3.3132

Nasir, S. N., Lee, C. D., Pea, R. & McKinney de Royston, M. (eds.). (2020). *Handbook of the Cultural Foundations of Learning.* Routledge.

Nattinger, J. & DeCarrico, J. (1992). *Lexical Phrases and Language Teaching.* Oxford.

Ngo, B. (2010). Doing "diversity" at Dynamic High: Problems and possibilities of multicultural education in practice. *Education and Urban Society. 42*(4), (pp. 473–495). https://doi.org/10.1177/0013124509356648

Nieto, S. (2018). *Language, Culture, and Teaching: Critical Perspectives* (3rd ed.). Routledge.

Nieto, S. & Bode, P. (2018). *Affirming Diversity: The Sociopolitical Context of Multicultural Education* (7th ed.). Pearson.

Olmedo, I. (2003). Accommodation and resistance: Latinas struggle for their children's education. *Anthropology & Education. 34*(4), (pp. 373–395).

Ong, W. J. (1982). *Orality and Literacy: The Technologizing of the Word.* Methuen.

Oyserman, D. (2017). Culture three ways: Culture and subcultures within countries. *Annual Review of Psychology. 68*, (pp. 435–463). https://doi.org/ 10.1146/annurev-psych-122414-033617

Packer, M. & Cole, M. (2022). The institutional foundations of human evolution, ontogenesis, and learning. Nasir, N. S., Lee, C.D., Pea, R. & McKinney de Royston, M. (eds.). (2020). *Handbook of the Cultural Foundations of Learning.* Routledge, (pp. 1–21).

Paradise, R. & Rogoff, B. (2009). Side by side: Learning by observing and pitching in: Cultural practices in support of learning. *Ethos. 37*, (pp. 102–138). https://doi.org/10.1111/j.1548-1352.2009.01033.x

Patterson, J., Hale, D. & Stessman, M. (2007/2008). Cultural contradictions and school leaving: A case study of an urban high school. *The High School Journal.* (Dec./Jan. 1–15). DOI: 10.1353/hsj.2008.0001

Paris, D. & Alim, H. S. (2014). What are we seeking to sustain through culturally sustaining pedagogy? A loving critique forward. *Harvard Educational Review. 84*(1), (pp. 85–100). https://doi.org/10.17763/haer.84.1.982l873k2 ht16m77

Paris, D. & Alim, H. S. (eds.). (2017). *Culturally Sustaining Pedagogies: Teaching and Learning for Justice in a Changing World.* Teachers College Press.

Pastoor, L. D. W. (2015). The mediational role of schools in supporting psychosocial transitions among unaccompanied young refugees upon resettlement in Norway. *International Journal of Development. 41*, (pp. 245–254). https://doi.org/10.1016/j.ijedudev.2014.10.009

Peregoy, S. & Boyle, O. (2022). *Reading, Writing and Learning in ESL: A Resource Book for Teaching K-12 English Learners* (8th ed.). Pearson.

Perry, K. H. (2008). From storytelling to writing: Transforming literacy practices among Sudanese refugees. *Journal of Literacy Research. 40*(3), (pp. 317–358). https://doi.org/10.1080/10862960802502196

Playsted, S. (2018). Finding their voice: Singing and teaching with refugees in Australia. *JALT Mind Brain Education Think Tanks. 4*(12). https://skyepl aystedtesol.files.wordpress.com/2020/07/finding-their-voice_-singing-and-teaching-with-refugees-in-austra.pdf

Popkewitz, T. S. (2013). Styles of reason: Historicism, historicizing, and the history of education. Popkewitz, T. S. (ed.). *Rethinking the History of Education.* Palgrave Macmillan, (pp. 1–28). DOI: 10.1057/9781137000705_1

Robinson, K. (2006, February). Do schools kill creativity? [Video]. TED Conferences. https://www.ted.com/talks/sir_ken_robinson_do_schools_kill_creativity?utm_campaign=tedspread&utm_medium=referral&utm_source=tedcomshare

Rogoff, B. (2014). Learning by observing and pitching in to family and community endeavors: An orientation. *Human Development. 57*(2–3), (pp. 69–81). https://doi.org/10.1159/000356757

Roofe, C. & Bezzina, C. (2018). *Intercultural Studies of Curriculum: Theory, Policy and Practice.* Palgrave Macmillan. https://doi-org.10.1007/978-3-319-60897-6

Ross, S. M. (2020). Technology infusion in K-12 classrooms: A retrospective look at three decades of challenges and advancements in research and practice. *Educational Technology and Research Development, 68,* 2003–2020. https://doi.org/10.1007/s11423-020-09756-7

Rotberg, I. (2004). Concluding thoughts: On change, tradition, and choices. Rotberg, I. (ed.). *Balancing Change and Tradition in Global Education Reform.* Rowman & Littlefield Education, (pp. 385–413).

Ryu, M. & Tuvilla, M. R. S. (2018). Resettled refugee youths' stories of migration, schooling, and future: Challenging dominant narratives about refugees. *Urban Review. 50*(4), (pp. 539–558). https://doi.org/10.1007/s11 256-018-0455-z

Salden, S. & Hertlein, J. (2020). Is it fair? The German education system and its stumbling blocks for adolescents. In Watzlawik, M. & Burkholder, A. (eds.). *Educating Adolescents Around the Globe: Becoming Who You Are in a World Full of Expectations.* Springer, (pp. 117–148).

Sahlström, J. F. (2002). The interactional organization of hand raising in classroom interaction. *Journal of Classroom Interaction. 37,* (pp. 47–57). https://www.jstor.org/stable/23870411

Salomon, F. & Apaza, E. C. (2006). Vernacular literacy on the Lake Titicaca High Plains, Peru. *Reading Research Quarterly. 41*(3), (pp. 304–326). https://doi.org/10.1598/RRQ.41.3.1

Samovar, L., Porter, R., McDaniel, E. & Roy, C. (eds.). (2014). *Intercultural Communication: A Reader* (14th ed.). Wadsworth.

Sanatullova-Allison, E. & Robison-Young, V. (2016). Overrepresentation: An overview of the issues surrounding the identification of English language learners with learning disabilities. *International Journal of Special Education. 31*(2). https://eric.ed.gov/?id=EJ1111073

Sarroub, L., Pernicek, T. & Sweeney, T. (2007). "I was bitten by a scorpion": Reading in and out of school in a refugee's life. *Journal of Adult Literacy. 50*(8), (pp. 668–679). https://doi.org/10.1598/JAAL.50.8.5

Saxe, G. B. (1998). Candy selling and math learning. *Educational Researcher. 17,* (pp. 14–21). http://www.jstor.org/stable/1175948

Scarino, A. (2019). The Australian curriculum and its conceptual bases: A critical analysis. *Curriculum Perspectives. 39*(8), (pp. 59–65). doi:10.1007/s41297-019-00066-4

Schleppegrell, M. (2004). *The Language of Schooling: A Functional Linguistics Perspective.* Lawrence Erlbaum.

Segal, E., Gerdes, K., Mullins, J., Wagaman, M. & Androff, D. (2011). Social empathy attitudes: Do Latino students have more? *Journal of Human Behavior in the Social Environment. 21*(4), (pp. 438–454). https://www.tandfonline.com/doi/abs/10.1080/10911359.2011.566445

Slavin, R. (2015). Cooperative learning in elementary schools. *International Journal of Primary, Elementary and Early Years Education. 43*(1), (pp. 5–14). https://doi.org/10.1080/03004279.2015.963370

Slavin, R. (2018). *Educational Psychology: Research and Practice* (12th ed.). Pearson.

Snow, M. A. & Brinton, D. (2019). *Content-Based Instruction: What Every ESL Teacher Needs to Know.* University of Michigan Press.

Snyder, S. C. & Fenner, D. S. (2021). *Culturally Responsive Teaching for Multilingual Learners: Tools for Equity.* Corwin.

Sousa, D. (2016). *How the Brain Learns* (5th ed.). Corwin.

Takyi-Amoako, E. J. & Assié-Lumumba, N. T. (2018). *Re-Visioning Education in Africa: Ubuntu-Inspired Education for Humanity.* Springer.

Taylor, E. V. (2012). Supporting children's mathematical understanding: Professional development focused on out-of-school practices. *Journal of Mathematics Teacher Education. 15,* (pp. 271–291). doi:10.1007/s10857-011-9187-7

Tonui, B. & Mitschke, D. (2020): "We still keep our culture to stay alive": Acculturation and adaptation among resettled young adult refugees from Burma. *Journal of Ethnic & Cultural Diversity in Social Work.* https://doi.org/10.1080/15313204.2020.1827334

Tourse, R. W. C., Hamilton-Mason, J., Wewiorski, N. J. (2018). *Systemic Racism in the United States.* Springer. https://link.springer.com/book/10.1007/978-3-319-72233-7

Tran, N. & Birman, D. (2017). Acculturation and assimilation: A qualitative inquiry of teacher expectations for Somali Bantu refugee students. *Education and Urban Society.* 51(5), (pp. 712–736). https://doi.org/10.1177/0013124517747033

Triandis, H. (1994). *Culture and Social Behavior.* McGraw Hill.

Triandis, H. (1995). *Individualism and Collectivism.* Westview Press.

Triandis, H. (2000). Culture and conflict. *International Journal of Psychology.* 35(2), (pp. 145–152). https://doi.org/10.1080/002075900399448

Trumbull, E., Greenfield, P., Rothstein-Fisch, C., Maynard, A., Quiroz, B. & Yuan, Q. (2020). From altered perceptions to altered practice: teachers bridge cultures in the classroom. *School Community Journal,* 30(1), (pp. 243–266). https://files.eric.ed.gov/fulltext/EJ1257613.pdf

Tyler, K., Uqdah, A., Dillihunt, M., Beatty-Hazelbaker, R., Conner, T., Gadon, N., Henchy, A., Hughes, T., Mulder, S., Owens, E., Roan-Belle, C., Smith, L. & Stevens, R. (2008). Cultural discontinuity: Toward a quantitative investigation of a major hypothesis in education. *Educational Researcher.* 37(5), (pp. 280–297). https://doi.org/10.3102/0013189X08321459

Van Allen, R. & Allen, C. (1967). *Language Experience Activities.* Houghton Mifflin.

Ventura, P., Pattamadilok, C., Fernandes, T., Klein, O., Morais, J. & Kolinsky, R. (2008). Schooling in Western culture promotes context-free processing.

Journal of Experimental Child Psychology. 100(2), (pp. 79–88). https://doi. org/10.1016/j.jecp.2008.02.001

Vincent, S. (2017). Transformations of collectivism and individualism in the Peruvian central Andes: A comunidad over three decades. *Ethnography. 19*(1), (pp. 63–83). https://doi.org/10.1177/1466138117713762

Vygotsky, L. (1978). *Mind in Society: The Development of Higher Psychological Processes.* Cole, M., John- Steiner, V., Scribner, S. & Souberman, E. (eds. & trans.). Harvard University Press. (Original work published 1934).

Walqui, A. (2006). Scaffolding instruction for English language learners: A conceptual framework. *International Journal of Bilingual Education and Bilingualism. 9*(2), (pp. 59–80). https://doi.org/10.1080/1367005060 8668639

Waring, H. Z. (2013). Managing competing voices in the second language classroom. *Discourse Processes. 50*(5), (pp. 316–338). https://doi.org/ 10.1080/0163853X.2013.779552

Waring, H. Z. (2016). *Theorizing Pedagogical Interaction: Insights From Conversation Analysis.* Routledge.

Watson, J. (2019). Understanding indigenous education practices as a way of engaging deeply with refugee-background students (and everyone else) in the classroom. *European Journal of Applied Linguistics and TEFL. 8*(1), (pp. 203–224). https://search-proquest-com.libdata.lib.ua.edu/docview/ 2343016164?accountid=14472

White, J. W. (2011). Resistance to classroom participation: Minority students, academic discourse, cultural conflicts, and issues of representation in whole class discussions. *Journal of Language, Identity, and Education. 10*(4), (pp. 250–265). doi.org/10.1080/15348458.2011.598128

Whitescarver, K. & Kalman, J. (2009). Extending traditional explanations of illiteracy: Historical and cross-cultural perspectives. *Compare. 39,* (pp. 501–515). DOI: 10.1080/03057920801903407

Willingham, D. (2009). *Why Don't Students Like School?* San Jossey-Bass.

Zhao, Y. (2016). From deficiency to strength: Shifting the mindset about education inequality. *Journal of Social Issues. 72*(4), (pp. 720–739).

Zwiers. J. (2013). *Building Academic Language: Essential Practices for Content Classrooms, Grades 5–12.* Jossey-Bass.

Index

Pages numbers followed by f indicates figure; t indicates table.

culture: collectivism, 13–14, 15–18, 16f, 29,
   38, 43; constructs of, 13–18; defined, 11–12;
   and educational systems, 23; iceberg model
   of, 11–12, 12f, 29; individualism, 14, 15–17,
   16f, 28, 29
curriculum: building associations in, 58–59,
   77, 86; as culturally relevant, 60; integration
   of MALP into, 120–22, 156–57

data analysis of class surveys, 137–38
data collection of class surveys, 146–47
debriefing phase of MALP projects, 149
decontextualized tasks: and class surveys, 127;
   and data analysis, 137; defined, 48; defining
   tasks, 117, 118–19; formal schema of, 66–67;
   and MALP, 73–75, 77, 89; and mathematical
   thinking, 96–97
deficit perspective of SLIFE, 37, 59, 167
defining tasks, 117, 118–19
differentiated instruction, 110, 127, 128–29, 159
display questions, 25–26
dropping out, 3, 18, 31, 69

education, culturally sustaining. See culturally
   sustaining education
education, Western-style. See formal education
"educational disadvantage," 37
educational systems, culture and, 23
effective instruction, 61
English, academic, 81

families, 14, 17–18
familismo, 17–18
fill-in-the-blank exercises, 124
formal education: and academic ways
   of thinking, 47–49; and activities for
   learning, 47t; assumptions of, 31–32; and
   components for learning, 35t, 49t; cooperative learning in, 42–43; core values of, 30t;
   cultural assumptions of, 27–30; defined,
   10, 24; literacy as central to, 18–23;
   processes for learning, 41t
formal schema, 33–34, 88
"funds of knowledge," 21, 60, 113

graphic organizers, 84
group learning. See cooperative learning
guided sentence practice, 119

heuristic thinking, 25
hierarchical cultures, respect for authority in, 29

higher order thinking skills (HOTS), 66
historical events, 147

ICF. See Intercultural Communication
   Framework (ICF)
immediate relevance. See relevance, immediate
independent learners, 29, 38–40. See also
   accountability, individual
individualistic cultures, 14, 15–17, 16f, 28, 29
interconnectedness: and class surveys,
   126, 133; in collectivistic cultures, 35, 38;
   and cultural dissonance, 39; and cultural
   perspectives projects, 153, 154; and differentiated classroom work, 110; and identifying
   priorities, 56; vs. independence, 35t, 38–40;
   and MALP, 68, 69–71; and math classes,
   94–95; and personal timelines, 147; vs.
   shared responsibility, 71–72; through
   projects, 86. See also communication,
   two-way; student-teacher relationships
Intercultural Communication Framework
   (ICF), 53–59, 68, 71, 77. See also communication, two-way; priorities, identifying
interdisciplinary approach of MALP
   projects, 156–57
internet as teaching tool, 88
intersectionality, 12
invisible culture, 11–12, 12f, 29

Jigsaw (cooperative activity), 42

KWL technique, 104, 131, 134

Language Experience Approach
   (LEA), 144–45
language schema, 75, 77, 88, 97, 127
learning, ways of, 23–27, 167–68,
   168f, 169
learning communities, 59, 60, 94, 110,
   113, 165
learning paradigms, 33, 34–35, 49, 49t, 64.
   See also activities for learning; conditions
   for learning; processes for learning
lesson snapshots, 101–5
Likert scale, 135
literacy, print: as "brought to life," 44–45;
   defined, 4; and extraction of meaning, 45–46;
   and formal education, 18–23, 24; and
   identifying priorities, 57
literacy skills: and self-esteem issues, 43; of
   SLIFE, 44t
lived experiences, 47t